Brand New Justice

For Anna

Brand New Justice

How branding places and products can help the developing world

Revised edition

Simon Anholt

ELSEVIER
BUTTERWORTH
HEINEMANN

AMSTERDAM • BOSTON • HEIDELBERG • LONDON • NEW YORK • OXFORD
PARIS • SAN DIEGO • SAN FRANCISCO • SINGAPORE • SYDNEY • TOKYO

Elsevier Butterworth-Heinemann
Linacre House, Jordan Hill, Oxford OX2 8DP
30 Corporate Drive, Burlington, MA 01803

First published 2003
Revised edition 2005

British Library Cataloguing in Publication Data
A catalogue record for this book is available from the British Library

Library of Congress Cataloguing in Publication Data
A catalogue record for this book is available from the Library of Congress

ISBN 0 7506 6600 5

For information on all Elsevier Butterworth-Heinemann publications visit
our website at http://books.elsevier.com

Typeset by Newgen Imaging Systems (P) Ltd, Chennai, India
Printed and bound in Great Britain

Working together to grow
libraries in developing countries

www.elsevier.com | www.bookaid.org | www.sabre.org

ELSEVIER   BOOK AID
            International   Sabre Foundation

Contents

Preface to the revised edition

For poor and developing countries trying to compete in the global marketplace, there is no shortage of well-intentioned help and advice on offer – cash and food aid, loans, technology and skills transfer, twinning, training and resource sharing ... the list is a long one, and it is a credit to the countries and organizations which offer the support that so much valuable help is on offer.

Yet one crucial item is missing from the list, a tool which none of the richer countries would be able to operate without, and a primary component of their remarkable economic success during the last century. This is their ability to *brand*.

Without brand value, capitalism could hardly exist – certainly not in its current form, providing enviable standards of living to hundreds of millions throughout the developed world. For branding is far more than a trick to sell more consumer goods at higher prices: it is part of the very foundations of competitiveness in a free marketplace, and with slight variations is to be found in education, in politics, in industry, in the labour market and throughout the public sector. Wherever an organization of any kind needs to compete and thrive in a busy environment, then brand value – lent by quality, by personality, by product or service superiority, by strategy – is what makes the difference.

The remarkable ability of branding to create, spread and sustain wealth throughout society means that any country which needs to improve its competitive edge should take a closer look at how it works, and the purpose of this book is to provide an introduction to branding as a tool for commercial, cultural and economic development.

Simon Anholt

CHAPTER 1

Why brands count

What I'm about to tell you is something you have probably heard before, but bear with me. It's an important introduction to what follows.

Here's how brands work:

On my left, a plastic bottle of sweet, fizzy brown fluid bearing the label 'Cola'. It cost me around 50 cents. On my right, a nearly identical bottle of sweet fluid bearing the label 'Coca-Cola'. It cost me just over a euro – or just over a dollar, if you prefer.

On my left, a good quality plain white tee-shirt. Cost: around ten euros. On my right, an identical white tee-shirt with a small Versace logo printed in black on the front. Cost: around 30 euros.

It seems almost criminal, doesn't it?

Well, that rather depends on who is doing it. This book explores the possibility that this phenomenon of branding, and certain other related techniques of wealth creation, could be better distributed around the world than they have been in the past. It shows how branding is, in fact, a powerful tool for economic development, and could make a very worthwhile contribution to the growth of the places which need it most.

Value you can't see

The brand value which marketing adds to products and services is not tangible value: unlike sales, products, factories, land, raw materials or workforces, you can't measure it very easily, but it represents capital because it enables producers and sellers to charge more money for their products and services and maintain a strong, long-term relationship with their customers. It is a multiplier of value, and as such, represents a substantial advantage for its owner: it's as good as money in the bank. You can borrow against it, buy it, sell it, invest in it, and increase or decrease it by good or bad management.

The concept of intangible value is a well established one in our capitalist system, and doesn't make brands any more suspect or less valid than any other form of commercial worth.

This additional value is not a trivial phenomenon; it forms a substantial part of the assets of the developed world. According to some estimates, brand value could be as much as one-third of the entire value of global wealth.

Being able to measure the value of these assets is clearly important, and Interbrand, a branding consultancy, have devised a widely-accepted method for doing this. According to their latest survey of the *Most Valuable Global Brands*, the intangible assets of the top 100 global brands are together worth $988 287 000 000: just a shade under a trillion dollars.

To put this almost unimaginably large number in context, it is roughly equal to the combined gross national income of *all* the 63 countries defined by the World Bank as 'low income' (and where almost half of the world's population lives).

Like me, you may find that a slightly disturbing thought, even though you've probably heard these kinds of statistics before. What can't be denied is that this elusive component of commerce is of great importance in understanding the distribution of wealth in the world today, and it is likely to have a role to play when we are trying to work out ways of balancing things better in the future.

There is little that is likeable about these mega-brands, the way they work, the companies which own them, or the fantastic quantities of wealth which they generate. But like it or not, rich and poor, we all live in a money-based global economy, and the lack of money is a primary cause of suffering: so it makes sense to take a closer look at how these brands multiply money, and see whether their genius for doing so might be transferable to some of the people and the places which *really* need it.

How brands create wealth

Selling products with well-known names, rather than bulk commodities or generic goods, has long been a smart business to be in.

Everybody knows that branded goods cost more than unbranded ones. You pay extra for the well-known name on your food, your clothing, your hi-fi, your running shoes, your car, and if you are one of those rather rare but very sensible people who always choose the supermarket-brand products, or products without well-known names at all, you will end up saving quite a lot of money.

But unless you're one of the brand rejecters, what do you actually get for the extra money you pay?

Well, although brand value is intangible, several aspects of the brand are of real value to the consumer; and much as some companies would like it to be so, a brand is not just a trick for overcharging consumers. Consumers aren't that stupid.

A product with a famous name is one you can usually depend on to do what it's meant to do, one that's made with quality ingredients or components, and backed by a substantial company which probably cares enough about its reputation to work hard to remedy any problems you may have with the product later on. A branded service business, one hopes, invests constantly in the best training for the best people. You can feel reasonably sure that a branded company will stay in business, in case you do have a problem with its products or service. Spare parts for branded products will be easy to find (although they will also be more expensive than the unbranded ones), and if you're really unhappy with the product, you can expect the company to take it back and refund your money. A brand is as much an open invitation to complain as it is a promise to deliver, and companies which deal lightly with complaints will soon erode their reputation.

So a brand also represents a considerable responsibility for its owner.

Brand names save shoppers time, effort and worry. Even though, in the rich countries of the northern hemisphere, it seems as if consumers spend rather too much of their lives either buying things or deciding which things to buy, few of us actually have the time, patience or expertise to research all of the minute differences between dozens or hundreds of competing products. To understand exactly why a BMW engine performs better or worse than a Mercedes engine, a Nike running shoe cushions better or worse than a Reebok, a Compaq is faster or slower than a Dell, you would need a degree in engineering.

A reputable brand enables us to shortcut this process: we feel we can take the quality, sophistication and reliability of the product on trust. The brand name is a promise that vast resources have been poured into making the product perform as well as the name implies. Most people feel that buying branded products is a safer bet, and don't mind paying well over the odds for this peace of mind: the higher price includes a contribution towards ensuring a better product from a better company.

In rich societies like North America, Western Europe and Japan, which largely revolve around acquisition, this ability of brands to reflect such attributes is so valuable that if the manufacturers didn't help consumers out by creating their own brands, the consumers would quickly find a way of investing their products with reputations themselves. If, by universal decree, Mercedes and BMW were compelled tomorrow to de-badge their cars, name them 'A' and 'B', and sell them at identical prices, it probably wouldn't be long before some consumers were boasting to their friends that they drove an A, and that this clearly made them rather classy – to the annoyance of B drivers, who would be equally convinced that their refined taste and discernment clearly marked them out as superior individuals.

Something like this once happened in the Soviet Union, where brands didn't exist. Soviet citizens quickly realised that the products in the state shops were produced in a variety of different factories, and each factory produced to its own quality standard. Within a very short time, shoppers had worked out how to read the barcodes on the products and tell where each product was made, and were thus able to exercise a kind of primitive brand selection.

It is often quite rightly pointed out in branding literature that companies don't invent or own their brands, consumers do. Reputation, after all, exists in the mind of the perceiver: it is not a quality of the product itself.

And of course there's the emotional side to branding, too. Like it or not, buying a branded product says something about you. At one very basic level, it is a way of showing people that you have enough money to pay more than strictly necessary for the things you own. Depending on the brand's image, it may also communicate something about the kind of person you are or would like people to think you are – your taste, your social standing and your attitudes. People have always used their possessions in this way, to express their wealth, taste and power: the addition of brand values to possessions simply makes them more expressive.

We are social animals with a keen sense of hierarchy, and most of us, rich and poor alike, are well prepared to pay extra for possessions which, in addition to or even instead of performing a useful function, advertise our status or act as badges for our various allegiances. Some brands – especially clothing brands – express our membership of cliques, schools of thought, ways of living; they express our attitudes towards authority, our mental age, our tastes and our political leanings. Rather usefully, the global brands even do this in a language which is international.

On the whole, our weakness in the West for the way brands work as badges is not something which we like to admit to: it's rather shaming to acknowledge that we are prepared to buy social status, or that we are foolish enough to spend more than necessary on a product which simply makes us feel or look a little better. Most of us would rather not confess how well our favourite brands pander to our weaker side, how intimately they know our secret vanities: we acknowledge them by buying them, but if asked directly, we may deny all knowledge of our real motivations. For the same reason, the whole system of branded products is easy to criticize, and there is always a ready audience for authors who criticize the way that brands work on us (often missing the point that they're only there because we want them to be).

And for the same reason, there has been a healthy market since the 1950's in America and Europe for fanciful books which reveal the dastardly tricks used by advertisers to coerce unwitting consumers into buying products they don't really want or need. We have always preferred to believe that we are being cynically manipulated by unknown forces than simply admit that we enjoy spending our money, and not always wisely.

Yet consumers for the most part subscribe voluntarily to their pact with brands, and their value in stimulating commerce, funding the media and generally creating wealth means that modern industrialized countries would sorely miss them if they went away. (One clear example of this is the calculation that if the London *Times* carried no advertising, it would cost nearly £21 per issue instead of its current cover price of around 60 pence.[1])

The same cannot be confidently said about consumers in less developed countries, where the pact is less equal, and where people are not so effectively 'immunized' against commercial messages from an early age. But more on this later.

All this is basic stuff, and we live in an age where most people – at least in the industrialized nations – are familiar with the mechanisms of brand image. In fact, it's interesting that, even though we all understand very well how brands work, and how at least part of what we're paying extra money for is really non-existent, we are still perfectly happy to carry on doing it. Some say this is foolishness; some call it decadence; some find it morally objectionable that so many people in the rich world will happily pay hundreds of euros for a pair of elegantly ripped and stained Diesel jeans whilst others go unclothed in Africa for want of a few cents' worth of cloth.

The real success story of branding in recent decades has been the way in which companies have used their brands to turn the satisfaction of complex and even spiritual needs into commercial transactions. Once people have reached a level of wealth where all their simple needs are fully met, where they lack nothing which is essential for the satisfactory continuation of their daily lives, one might imagine that their surplus time and energy would then be expended on fulfilling higher, spiritual and intellectual needs. One might also imagine that commerce has no part to play in this pursuit.

But as people in richer countries have moved beyond basic wants, so companies have kept pace with their increasingly complex and intangible desires, attaching the promise of status, peer approval, tranquillity, happiness, wisdom, intelligence, sex appeal, long life, fitness, youthfulness, to their branded products. Now that every desire in our waking lives is fulfilled, brands manage to sell us our dreams. Brands continue to exist and generate huge profits because that is the only way in which consumers who own everything they want can be stimulated to carry on consuming as if they still needed things.

There is rather more to achieving these spiritual ends than owning the accessories which go with them, or the brands which reflect the lifestyle which matches them: so, like drinking salt water when you're thirsty, the brands do little more than sharpen the desire without ever satisfying it. This may all sound a little pious, but I think most readers in rich or developing countries will know the ache of wanting and wanting a particular possession, at last buying it, and then feeling the same emptiness gradually return a few days or weeks later.

This may partly explain the rapid growth of FairTrade products and well-marketed charity appeals: they enable us to spend money without feeling cheapened or impoverished afterwards. I mention this sensation because it has some relevance to the arguments which follow in this book.

How brands distribute wealth

So the branding mechanism keeps running, and continues to create wealth. The fact that the system is so pervasive and so durable doesn't necessarily mean that it's healthy or even morally sound, but it does suggest that it responds to something pretty real in human nature.

Brands remain economically attractive because enough people believe that they are worth paying extra for: the companies which are lucky and clever enough to own powerful brands make more money than the companies which don't, and some of the extra money which consumers pay for extra brand appeal is pure profit for the brand-owner. This is why company bosses are sometimes quoted as saying that their brand names are worth more than the rest of their business assets put together: you have to keep investing in your brand, and your product and customer service have to live up to the promise of the name, but when it's in good health, a brand is a licence to charge more money for your products.

Although increased profitability is one of the main attractions of being a brand-owner, it isn't all about margin. The large consumer brands may enjoy 15–20 per cent greater margins than producers which aren't household names, but the real benefit for the brand-owner occurs over time. Brands represent *sustainable wealth*: it's the loyalty of the consumer base, the ready acceptance of new products launched under the same name, and the relative cheapness of retaining loyal customers compared to the cost of continually finding new ones which really makes the difference, and enables branded businesses to grow exponentially over time.

One survey has even revealed the startling fact that brand leaders, far from getting locked into an ever-increasing spiral of marketing costs to sustain their brand images, actually spend *less* on advertising than their competitors.[2] (The corollary of this, of course, is that the competitors need to spend more, so the advertising industry is in little danger of doing itself out of a job).

In the longer term, brands create wealth around themselves. The additional profit margin means that the company can invest more money in research and development to maintain the flow of innovative, high quality new products to market; in marketing to maintain and enhance the profile and power of its brands and keep up with the market leaders; in people and systems to improve its customer service.

This enriches the substantial service sector which surrounds the makers and marketers of products. As they grow, the companies employ more and more people, buy more raw materials, use yet more services, build more factories and offices, and pay more taxes. Their distributors and retailers benefit from bigger sales, and share in the bigger profits, which means more companies hiring more people and engaging more service businesses, retailers expanding their businesses to meet the growing demand from consumers, and all *these* companies paying more taxes too.

Research from the USA showing figures for direct and indirect employment by large companies[3] suggests that the employment effect within clusters centred around a major international brand can be dramatic: Dell Computer's Texas operations, for example, employ 12 500 people directly, but are responsible for creating some 30 000 jobs in total; 3M directly employs 20 000 workers in Minnesota, creating 54 280 total jobs; Monsanto directly employs 3 800 people in Missouri, and creates 9 650 jobs. In other words, each of these companies is creating between two and a half and three times as many jobs for the local economy as actually appear on its payroll.

Gradually, wealth spreads out from successful companies, merges with the wealth spreading out from successful supporting and competing companies in the same region, and it stimulates the economy of the city, the region, and ultimately the country in which the company is based.

Life on the lower tier

The brand effect is one of the ways in which the countries which had already generated great wealth through trade and empire-building in the previous three or four centuries have managed to become richer still during the last hundred years.

Today, many big corporations acknowledge that their real expertise is in product design and marketing, and this is where they invest most heavily. The less profitable parts of their enterprise, such as sourcing the basic raw materials, manufacturing and finishing the products, are farmed out to wherever they can get the required quality for the lowest price – and it's almost invariably in the second or third world.

These companies no longer need to produce or manufacture: all they need to do is brand and deliver, and the money comes rolling in.

Companies in emerging and third-world countries, on the whole, haven't been able to do this trick, and still make most of the foreign income which is so crucial to their economies through supplying companies in rich countries with the raw materials or basic manufactured goods and labour they need.

But these supplies, since they are unbranded, are generally identical to those of their many competitors, are extremely price-sensitive, and generate very slender profits indeed.

In addition to their Top 100 global brands survey which I mentioned at the beginning of this chapter, Interbrand also publish rankings and valuations of Brazil's top 12 brands (none of which have significant sales outside Brazil or are worth anywhere near a billion dollars, so of course don't make it into the Global Top 100).

The combined value of these local heroes is just over $4 billion (the top 12 US brands are worth somewhat more than 100 times as much). Their value compares very differently to the country's income, as well: Brazil's top 12 equate to less than half a percent of GNI, whereas America's top 12 are nearer 5 per cent. Massive reserves of intangible wealth would appear to be a characteristic of the healthy, modern economy. Whether this is something we should be concerned about, I leave to others to decide.

As it stands, most poorer countries are enmeshed in various patterns of behaviour which keep them poor, and one of these is selling unbranded goods to richer nations at low margins. Companies in the richer nations then add large amounts of margin to the goods by finishing, packaging, branding, and retailing them to the end user. The poor country's part in this process often helps to deplete its resources while keeping its foreign revenues at a break-even level or below.

The margins on this kind of transaction have been compressed even further in recent decades as globalization has advanced, making life as a 'supplier nation' an increasingly unattractive proposition. As time passes, the profits at the branding end of business grow, and there is a tendency for the profits at the supplier end to shrink.

Before globalization reached today's levels, being a supplier nation did provide opportunities for reasonably stable foreign income, even if it was seldom a recipe for great wealth. But in a globally networked world, where brand-owning companies are free to shop around the world for their raw materials, their manufacturing and labour, and instantaneously locate the best combination of sufficient quality and low price, supplying them has become an extremely risky business.

Instead of suppliers in poor countries competing on a local level for contracts to supply rich companies in the North, they are now in direct and constant competition with other suppliers all over the world. Farmers in one country may have a less favourable climate with a shorter growing season; and a single poor crop may make it almost impossible to win back contracts in subsequent years. An American or European company can switch its suppliers of raw materials from Latin America to South-East Asia overnight if the price is right. Suppliers in Thailand can bid on the internet for contracts against suppliers in Kenya and Peru, and this creates a very volatile situation: in some countries, factories and producers may enjoy massive government subsidies, international aid or development grants and thus drop their prices way below anything the rest can afford, or they may have a cheaper labour force and thus undercut the rest. World Bank concessional loans for supporting Vietnamese coffee production, for example, have all but wiped out the robusta coffee business of several African countries: in a globalized world, it's almost impossible to help one country without harming another.

The consequence of this effect of globalization is more and more intense competition between supplier nations, which means greater risks and ever tighter margins for the suppliers, and better and better opportunities for the purchasing companies in the West. It's no business for the faint-hearted.

Isn't it the poor world's turn?

A visitor from another planet might well ask, if poorer countries want to do something to catch up, why don't they simply play the same game, and encourage their industries to start selling finished, branded goods direct to consumers rather than unbranded goods and materials to brand-owners? If one third of the entire world's wealth is composed of this thing called brand value, why aren't poorer countries getting into the branding business too?

After all, for an emerging market, branded exports would represent *protected margin*: unlike commodities and labour, which depend entirely on price, quality and timely delivery in order to maintain preference, successfully branded goods can – at least for a while – keep their customer base even after all other factors have been erased. Buyers return endlessly, willingly, sometimes almost automatically to the companies which produce their favourite brands, and will always take an interest in and give preference to new, unknown products from the same companies. Of course, companies can also show preference towards long-standing suppliers with a history of efficient service, and this is like a weak form of brand loyalty, but since the offering itself generally has nothing to distinguish it from any other on the market apart from price, that loyalty may be short-lived if a cheaper alternative appears.

If it is true that branding is simply adding a range of intangible attributes to a quality product, and since so many of the quality products are already manufactured in emerging markets, there is little question that graduating from commodities or unbranded manufactures to brands would be a highly effective way for companies in such countries to improve their income and profits – and, perhaps, if enough companies did it, to improve the wealth of the entire country as well.

There is much simple justice in this idea, and a simple formula is irresistible. I raised the following point at the end of my last book, and it forms the opening thought of this one:

- If a company in a rich country sells brands to rich consumers in the same or other rich countries, nothing really happens: money simply circulates within a more or less closed system, and there's little to criticize on moral grounds.
- If a company in a rich country sells brands to poor consumers in the same or other rich countries, there is a risk of exploitation and a further widening of the wealth gap.
- If a company in a rich country sells brands to consumers in a poor country, the risk of exploitation is far higher.
- But if a company in a poor country sells brands to consumers in a rich country, the overall balance begins to be redressed, and justice begins to be done.

So why doesn't it happen?

Conventional wisdom says that companies in poor countries can't get rich by exporting branded goods and services for several reasons. These are the five most common ones:

1. they can't produce high enough quality products or services;
2. they can't afford to promote or distribute them internationally;
3. they don't have the expertise to build international brands;
4. even if they did, nobody in rich countries would want to buy them;
5. even if they did, and even if people did buy them, the resulting profits would never benefit the economy as a whole, and would simply disappear into the pockets of a few corrupt individuals.

In this book are some responses to these five objections, as well as an exploration of the consequences of rejecting them, and some thoughts on how governments and producers in developing countries might take advantage of the potential of branding for their own progress and development.

Branding the exports, branding the nation

The starting-point of *Brand New Justice* is that companies in many poorer countries *can and do* develop and sell their own branded goods and services abroad. What's more, they can sell them not just in other poor countries, but in many cases back to the rich countries which until now have been their 'clients', and so control more of the commercial process – and the profits – from conception through to sale.

This kind of business is also good for the country where such companies are based. Companies with successful export brands provide an example and an inspiration to other companies, they generate national pride and prosperity in their immediate neighbourhood, and perhaps above all they make foreign consumers and investors think again about their country: a place which is capable of producing attractive, desirable, high-quality exports is a place worthy of some respect. It may even be worth visiting; it certainly makes other products from the same country worth a look.

More branded export business is most certainly a step in the right direction for an emerging country. But unless the companies are big or numerous enough in proportion to the country to represent a meaningful slice of national income, and unless there are fair and reliable ways to ensure that their profits don't vanish exclusively into private hands, then showing a few companies how to improve their profit margins won't have any major, immediate impact on the development of the whole country.

But branding has a far bigger role to play than this.

If the development of these export brands is supported and encouraged by government, and written as a key component into a consistent, imaginative and well-managed *national* brand strategy, it can make a real difference to the country's long-term prospects.

A national brand strategy determines the most realistic, most competitive and most compelling strategic vision for the country, and ensures that this vision is supported, reinforced and enriched by *every* act of communication between the country and the rest of the world.

Those acts of communication include the kinds of brands which the country exports; the way it promotes itself for trade, tourism, inward investment and inward recruitment; the way it behaves in acts of domestic and foreign policy and the ways in which these acts are communicated; the way it promotes and represents and shares its culture; the way its citizens behave when abroad and how they treat strangers at home; the way it features in the world's media; the bodies and organizations it belongs to; the countries it associates with; the way it competes with other countries in sport and entertainment; what it gives to the world and what it takes back.

If done well, such a strategy can make a huge difference to both the internal confidence and the external performance of a country. Image and progress unfailingly go hand in hand, and although it is usually true that image is the consequence of progress, rather than vice versa, it is equally true that when *both* are carefully managed in tandem, they help each other along and create accelerated change.

It is an approach which concentrates as much on the representation of actions as on the actions themselves. This is because the first lesson which marketing has to teach is that other people are less interested in you than *you* are, so if you care about what they think, it's your responsibility to make yourself properly understood. Marketing teaches us that people are just as often guided by their perceptions of things as by the reality of things. Good marketers know that being in possession of the truth is not sufficient – people still need to be persuaded that it's the truth.

Indeed, one could well argue that since public perceptions of government actions are so critical to their success or failure, it is actually irresponsible behaviour if a government fails to consider the perceptual implications of its actions, and the investments it makes on behalf of its taxpayers.

Marketing also teaches that people can't be deceived for long; that the higher you raise their expectations, the more completely they reject your offering when they are disappointed; and you can't make people buy a bad product more than once. So every good marketer knows that his or her primary responsibility is to ensure that the product matches up to the promise, because misleading marketing is ineffective marketing.

Edward R. Murrow, the Director of the United States Information Agency, echoed this principle when he testified before a Congressional Committee in 1963:

> American traditions and the American ethic require us to be truthful, but the most important reason is that truth is the best propaganda and lies are the worst. To be persuasive we must be believable; to be believable we must be credible; to be credible we must be truthful. It is as simple as that.

All this sounds to most people like pretty good sense, but in some countries the vocabulary is sadly inflammatory. My own country, Britain, is an acute example of this: there is a widespread, strong, perhaps idealistic or even naïve feeling that public affairs and international relations are, or should be, purely about deeds and facts; marketing, on the other hand, is seen by many as a dirty and unprincipled business, dealing with surface and illusion, vanity and deception: lies, in short. Politics is about actions, marketing about hot air. (The most frequently heard criticism of our present government is that they are too concerned about how they are regarded. In many countries, this would be considered a rather mild complaint, but in the UK it is a serious charge.)

Wherever you go, branding places is an emotive subject. Somehow, when the fiendish tricks of marketing are applied to something as sacred as the nation-state, all hell breaks loose. Insults are heaped on the heads of brands, marketers and policy-makers alike – 'spin', 'gloss' and 'lies' are the most commonly heard in this country. In my own work, helping to improve the prospects of emerging markets through better branding of the country and its products, I am often accused of 'rewriting history', 'social engineering', 'cultural pollution', 'exploitation', 'condescension', 'neo-imperialism', and worse.

But of course countries have been branding themselves systematically and deliberately for many centuries: what appears to bother people is simply the vocabulary. So I am well aware that putting the words 'brand' and 'nation' in the same sentence is guaranteed to raise hackles; and I am equally aware that my attempts to defuse the debate may, at least in Britain, be a waste of breath.

Most intelligent observers of world affairs understand that the success and influence of countries is always composed of a balance between what Joseph Nye, a political scientist, calls 'soft' and 'hard' power. There are times when only coercion can achieve the aims which a government, rightly or wrongly, wishes to pursue, and this is hard power; other ends can only be attained through the exercise of cultural, intellectual or spiritual influence – as Nye says, 'a country may obtain the outcomes it wants in world politics because other countries want to follow it, admiring its values, emulating its example, aspiring to its level of prosperity and openness.'[4] Soft power, he says, is making people *want* to do what you want them to do. National branding is about making people *want* to pay attention to a country's achievements, and believe in its qualities. It is the quintessential modern exemplar of soft power.

The implications of Nye's theory for my argument are clear: you can only wield hard power over countries which lie beneath you in the hierarchy of nations. For emerging countries, which lie beneath the rest, the only power which they can hope to wield is soft.

The vocabulary is immaterial: one can call these principles of soft power 'marketing' or 'branding', but one can equally call them psychology, diplomacy, rhetoric, politics, the art of persuasion, or plain good sense.

What matters is whether they work or not. And they do work.

Global brands from emerging markets

The export brands of emerging countries are a good starting-point, and the first half of this book concentrates on them.

Experience shows that nation-branding programmes seldom achieve anything useful, or even get off the ground, unless they are backed by solid commitment by both government and exporting companies. Brands also have a particular power to accelerate and lead changes in the public perceptions of countries: as I will describe in Chapter 5, commercial brands, whether we like it or not, are increasingly important vectors of national image and reputation, even of culture.

For the last eight years, I've been trawling the developing world for examples of companies which are exporting their own products under their own names, and have seen enough of them – over 200, at the time of writing – to believe that this phenomenon is rapidly spreading, and in some cases is likely to become, or is already, of great significance to the prospects of the country where the brands are produced.

In Chapter 3, I will describe some of the emerging market entrepreneurs who, often against great odds, are succeeding in becoming brand-owners; in many cases, the rapid growth of their businesses tells its own story.

- a Thai sweatshop which has started to export its own branded garments (and making many times the profit it did when it manufactured for American brands);
- a Mumbai chemicals company which is taking on the Parisian fashion houses at the perfume game, and winning;
- the Hong Kong businessman making a global fortune out of Chinese chic;
- the Russian entrepreneur who has created a premium international vodka brand and now wants to follow it up with banking services and become Russia's answer to Richard Branson;
- Infosys, which is making Bangalore the global capital of IT services;
- the Czech furniture business which markets itself with art, and is taking on the multinational giants.

There are enough failures, too, to remind us of the fragility of this phenomenon, and the daunting barriers which face anyone bold enough to try: Chapter 4 deals with some of the difficulties which are commonly encountered, and suggests some solutions, as well as outlining the positive lessons we can learn from the examples described in the previous chapter.

Chapter 5 is dedicated to giving a proper answer to the fourth objection listed above (*even if they did, nobody in the West would want to buy them*). Through an analysis of the practice and theory of managing a country's brand, this chapter shows how proper management of national image can make a real difference to the global competitiveness of a country, region or city.

Every marketing idea must begin by looking at the customer, and Chapter 6 explores some of the current trends in taste and popular culture which clearly show that many consumers in the developed world are quite ready to buy global brands from emerging markets. Chapter 6 also frames some of the questions raised but left unanswered in this book, and proposes an agenda for further study, discussion and action.

Making it happen

One thing needs to be stressed at this point. The basic concept of *Brand New Justice* is aimed more at transition economies in the 'second world' than at the least developed countries. It is certainly worthwhile debating whether the same arguments can be usefully applied to the very poorest and chronically indebted countries, and some interesting work is being done which seems to prove that there are benefits to be achieved in this area, especially in the field of place branding (I will touch on this in Chapter 6), but it is not the primary focus of the book.

In most LDCs, the companies able to 'fast-track' to becoming brand-owners simply don't exist, and the only sensible national communications strategy is to generate immediate aid and investment. If a country isn't able to provide food and shelter for its population, or if its main problems are disease, illiteracy and war, then talk of enhancing the image of its exports and of the country itself would be, to say the least, misplaced.

Creating a branded export business requires many conditions to be in place: companies which are competent to manufacture to the standards required by consumers in whichever market they are sold; a legal and financial system which makes manufacturing and exporting feasible, enables the company to offer reliable deliveries of its products abroad, and allows people who make a legal profit to hold onto it; a national IT and telecoms infrastructure which enables the company to 'plug in' to the global economy; a stable and business-friendly government with fair and consistent taxation policies; a reliable supply of raw materials; a labour force with the necessary skills and creativity; astable currency and a dependable banking sector; access to sources of capital; and the list goes on.

Planning a national branding strategy also requires certain conditions: the political resource and will to collaborate fully, fairly and transparently with the private sector; a feasible and coherent plan of economic and social development which can form the basis of the place-brand strategy; sufficient goodwill and trust with companies, organizations, local and regional government, city authorities, the civil service, trades unions, the tourist board and the population at large to create widespread acceptance of the strategy; and a degree of basic financial stability. Perhaps most importantly, the project needs the personal backing of the 'Chief Executive' of the country, whoever he or she may be, otherwise it is unlikely to achieve anything lasting.

Justice being done

It will become plain during the course of this book that despite having worked for twenty years in advertising, marketing and branding – or perhaps because of it – I am not an uncritical admirer of the capitalist system or a wholesale supporter of globalization in all its manifestations.

However, these techniques of marketing are the ones which I know well enough to appreciate their power to do good, and my hope is that in sharing these thoughts, some of this wasted power can be harnessed.

Part of the reason why the central idea of *Brand New Justice* appeals to me is because it also represents an opportunity for my own industry to do itself some credit, and undo some of the harm that it has done during the past century.

Until recently, by and large, this harm has been done innocently. But for at least the last fifteen years, anyone who has claimed that helping first-world companies to increase their profits is just a job like any other, and has nothing to do with ethics, is being highly disingenuous, and treading on rather thin ice.

Yet many marketers do so, and it may be one of the reasons why the industry is having increasing difficulty in attracting graduates of the quality who, ten or fifteen years ago, were queuing up at its doors. In the new moral and ethical climate in which we find ourselves, a company which can only justify its existence in terms of increasing shareholder value may well find that recruiting people who are good (in every sense of that interesting word) becomes more and more of a problem.

Brand New Justice is not a solution to all the world's problems, and it's certainly not the only solution to any part of them. But its implications are, I believe, significant: sharing wealth means sharing the access routes to wealth, and it would be a fine thing if marketing could help to show the way.

The critics of globalization are rightly perturbed by the idea of rich countries using their brands to create 'consumerist desires' in poorer countries which the inhabitants of those countries can't afford to satisfy. My modest proposal is that we should seek for ways to reverse the model: let the entrepreneurs and workers in poorer countries create the desires in the minds of consumers who *can* afford to satisfy them.

The fact is that we can't have it both ways. Either marketing works, and it is a powerful tool for change, in which case it must admit responsibility for the absolutely central role it has played in creating the ever-widening inequality between rich and poor during the last century; or else it is nothing, and has enriched itself over the decades without giving any value in return, and can play no useful part in the huge tasks which lie ahead for humanity in the next century.

CHAPTER 2

What brands do for countries

There are many different ways of telling the economic history of the world, and there have been many different explanations for how some fairly small and apparently unpromising countries managed to become extremely rich, while other large and fertile lands have never managed to drag themselves above the level of subsistence.

Some versions of economic history are based on an overtly Eurocentric, almost supremacist view that Europeans basically invented capitalism and so they and their descendants are, by cultural and historical decree, the only people capable of practising it. (There are also plenty of predictions that the 'Anglo-Saxon' model of capitalism will eventually prevail as globalization completes its relentless advance.) Other accounts take the more balanced and altogether more interesting approach that the current state of affairs is little more than a happy (for some) accident of history, and might easily be altered or reversed in a different age, under different prevailing circumstances. Some people think that it's climate, some think it's culture, and some think that whatever the reasons are, it's no bad thing.

One of the most interesting contributions to the discussion was made by Hernando de Soto,[5] whose observations remind us not to confuse capitalism with commerce: capitalism is simply the (highly productive) version of commerce which Western countries have practised andperfected, but this doesn't mean that Western countries have a monopoly on entrepreneurship, creativity, competitive spirit, ambition, salesmanship or even greed. Commerce has been around for millennia, and in fact has usually been considered a more respectable pursuit, sometimes even a princely one, in the East than in the West.

It is, argues de Soto, the complex and peculiarly Western system of legally-protected property title which has enabled trade in the West to burgeon into capitalism on a major scale, and the lack of such a system which keeps the great wealth of parts of the 'undeveloped' world in unmeasurable, non-negotiable and unrealizable form (you can't take out a mortgage, for example, against a property for which you hold no formal legal title). The argument clearly has its application on the issue of brands: without the protection afforded by intellectual property legislation, and the right of a manufacturer to protect its namestyle, it would be impossible for the value of a brand name to be considered a quantifiable asset of the business: and the market capitalisation of a company like Xerox, for example, would be a mere $481 million rather than six-and-a-half billion dollars.[6]

Western traders have simply been more imaginative and elastic in their view of what constitutes a token or symbol of value, as well as more rigorous in their system of capturing and protecting these symbols. Brands, as I noted in the first chapter, are just another proxy for negotiable wealth, and, like many such symbols which are commonplace and universally recognized in the developed economies, have little or no currency in the poorer world, where money and goods are still the primary vehicles of value.

The notion of adding 'intangible' value to products in order to justify charging a higher price, or at least in order to ensure a stronger and longer hold over as many purchasers as possible, is as old as commerce itself. Advertising materials designed to reassure consumers of the extra quality or desirability of a particular company's products have been found by archaeologists in ancient Egyptian, Greek and Roman cities. The moment consumers have a choice, brand names start to count.

The basic principles of creating, communicating and protecting the reputation which those names embody were already well established in the Middle Ages, as the example of the early Italian banking companies shows. Some would argue that there has been relatively little additional progress in the field since then.

The first pan-European brands

In Italy, certain family names emerged early in the fourteenth century as symbols of wealth, trust and integrity: the Buonsignori of Siena – the first major international bank – then the Frescobaldi of Florence, the Ricciardi of Lucca, and later still, the Bardi, Peruzzi and Acciaiuoli families, some of whose business empires employed hundreds of staff in subsidiary offices across Europe and the Middle East and North Africa[7] – the area which modern multinational companies call EMEA.

Century after century, other Italian families have followed in this trading tradition. The first family brands whose names a modern consumer would recognize begin to appear in the sixteenth century with families like Beretta, which was arguably the first pan-European consumer goods brand. Beretta took their first order on 3rd October 1526 (for 185 blunderbusses at 296 ducats)[8] and are still a leading global firearms brand, as their website, www.beretta.com, testifies.

The story of Italian family brands continues today with names like Benetton, Armani, Gucci, Prada, Ferrari, Moto Guzzi, Bertolli, Laverda, Barilla, Ferrero, Olivetti, Martini, Peroni, Fiorucci, Pirelli, Stefanel, Buitoni, Versace, Lamborghini, Maserati and Bugatti: several of these companies have been trading for centuries. It is noticeable that almost all of the Italian brands which are internationally renowned fall into three product categories: motor vehicles; fashion and luxury goods; and food and drink. Whether this concentration of reputation is the result of a concentration of expertise, or vice-versa, will be discussed more fully in Chapter 5.

In their correspondence and journals, the medieval Italian merchants stress over and over again the importance of creating a good and famous name: to be recognized far and wide as honourable citizens, to play a distinguished part in social and civic life, to support culture and donate to good causes. It's most interesting how this aspect of corporate reputation, never forgotten or overlooked by most clever and successful companies, has recently recaptured the attention of big business, and the idea has been relaunched and rebranded as 'corporate social responsibility' or 'corporate citizenship', as if it were something that had just been invented.

Only an impeccable reputation for probity, substantial resources and success could automatically confer the kind of trust among new clients which ensured the continuation of their business. In every respect, the power of these family names was identical to modern brands: they acted as a shortcut to an informed buying or investing decision, and stood as a universally-acknowledged proxy for dependability.

Ever since the publication of what was probably the first ever international business best-seller, the snappily-titled *Book of Knowledge of the Beauties of Commerce and of Cognisance of Good and Bad Merchandise and of Falsifications*, written by Abu al-Fadl Ja'far Ibn Ali of Damascus some time between the ninth and twelfth centuries, it has been understood that one's good name is worth more than riches, for the simple reason that it is the necessary basis for continued enrichment. People will only buy from people whom they know and trust, but as soon as trade extends beyond the limits of close acquaintances – which of course it must, if larger fortunes are to be made – then one's good name must somehow be broadcast, and become a byword for trustworthiness. Hence the value of reputation: it is the broadcast of trust. Reputation is the means by which 'consumers' and other 'business-to-business purchasers' will feel reasonably safe about doing business with you even if they have never met you before.

In exactly the same way as non-locally-produced products need brand-names based on a reputation for quality in order to stand in for personal experience, so trading families – the 'service brands' of their day – needed brand names based on a reputation for honour as soon as their circle of trade extended beyond the home town or a day's travel. Brands are a necessary consequence of the growing distance between buyer and seller; and this distance is a necessary function of the desire to expand the business to benefit from a wider marketplace.

How profit comes from polarization

In the early days of international trade, that first great profit of the wealthy nations was often built on a simple market distortion: companies benefited from transporting a product from a country where it was plentiful, and selling it in a country where it was scarce. In other cases, the profits were made on buying cheaply, or plundering, raw ingredients from poorer countries, manufacturing them into finished goods, and selling these on to what we now call 'end users'.

Thus, for example, the wealth of cities like Venice, Genova, Amalfi and Pisa were originally built in the Middle Ages by traders who bought pepper, spices and other goods in Alexandria, Palestine, Syria and North Africa, and sold them on at a vast profit to other European distributors, resellers and consumers; centuries later, long after other European powers had made their own expeditions to the East and destroyed the monopolies of Venice and the other Italian city-states, England, Holland, Portugal, Spain, France, Germany and Belgium were following pretty much the same process. The British Empire was started by a corporation – the East India Company – and only after 257 years completed its transition from private sector enterprise to governance.

There was little call for brand value in these transactions, since the rare produce and treasured delicacies which the trading companies obtained from far-flung places effectively sold themselves: the seller had a virtual monopoly on the supply of the product. But globalization has continued its advance (barring a few checks and reversals) since the Middle Ages, and the opportunities for purveying a product which is genuinely unique, or for enjoying any kind of monopoly for more than a few weeks at a time, are increasingly rare.

Consumers in all but the poorest or most isolated countries are now faced with product parity in most sectors, and a wide choice of competing products. So brands have risen in importance, and the value of a company's reputation has become a more and more fundamental part of its ability to stay competitive and stay in business.

The way in which companies now structure their operations fully reflects this increasing emphasis on intangible competitiveness.

During the second half of the last century, companies in the rich world began to outsource not only the supply of raw materials and labour, but also the manufacturing and finishing of merchandise to poorer countries where overheads are lower. They concentrated and clustered their expenditure and expertise ever closer to the extreme ends of the value chain – what you might call the 'first and last mile' to the consumer – right at the beginning (where research, development and design of new products and new technologies takes place), and right at the end (where brand value and differentiation are added to the finished article). In this way, companies could harness the superior education and training, creativity, design and marketing skills which were still largely the monopolies of the North, whilst benefiting from the cheapness of unskilled labour and basic materials in the South.

And if they rationalize their input beyond this extreme degree of polarization, companies will always give up the first mile rather than the last, outsourcing the conception and design of their products to suppliers in developing countries. Some American and European fashion brands, for example, now allow their Asian suppliers to design many of the individual garments in their ranges; the brand-owner's input at this stage of the process is reduced to conceiving new ranges and placing the orders. Likewise, only the biggest global electronics brands maintain their own R&D and design facilities, the others preferring to select ready-made and unbranded new products from permanent trade shows in Taipei which they re-badge, import, promote and sell.

In this way, the already rich companies, and the already rich countries in which they are headquartered, have pulled ever further away from the poorer countries which supply them with cheap products, cheap labour – and, of course, with consumers. These consumers don't have all that much money, but they are plentiful and willing, and often have a powerful desire to buy into a fragment of the image of the first-world brands and the rich countries whose image they appear to reflect.

There is a familiar pattern which has been repeated over and over again during the last hundred years: a company from an industrialized nation invests in a poorer nation as a manufacturing resource, and then uses it as a market for its products. It's a highly effective strategy, and has created huge fortunes for many thousands of companies in Europe and North America; and, of course, the benefits for the host country can also be substantial. In some cases, such as Ireland in the twentieth century, foreign direct investment could literally save the country from ruin (Figure 2.1).

And of course, the detailed picture is by no means so simple, and many billions of dollars' worth of raw materials also travel in the opposite direction, exported by the industrialized nations to be processed in other developed economies as well as poorer countries. But on the

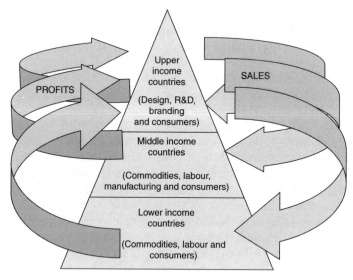

Figure 2.1   Global value flows

whole, there is a clear polarization of roles in the modern world: the upper income countries are primarily in the intellectual property and 'value-adding' game: they are the designers and brand owners. The middle-income countries are their manufacturing base and cheap source of semi-skilled labour; and the third world is the bargain-basement supplier of raw materials. All these countries, of course, form the marketplace for the products which the system produces; and the vast bulk of the profit is retained by the rich countries.

Where this leaves the poorer countries

The assumption that these roles are fixed and immutable is rarely questioned. The highest hope to emerge from the Doha round of the WTO was a promise to make it easier for poorer countries to sell their *agricultural products* and *textiles* to wealthy countries – an essential promise indeed, since these are in many cases their only output – but the emphasis and the expectation remains firmly on the South continuing to act as supplier and manufacturer to the developed world. There is no talk of the client/supplier relationship ever altering.

The middle-income countries – those whose per capita income falls roughly between $750 and $10 000 per year, and whose population accounts for around 85 per cent of the world's total – benefit from the global pattern to the extent that their economies are, very gradually, becoming less and less dependent on the wild vacillations of agricultural and commodity exports, and an ever greater proportion of their income derives from the export of manufactured goods – a more profitable and somewhat more stable business. In this sense, globalization works in their favour.

By 2000, these countries accounted for 27 per cent of world exports of manufactures, a remarkable increase from their 17 per cent share only ten years before. Exports of office and telecoms equipment alone accounted for a larger share of their exports than either agricultural or mining products. Somewhere between two-thirds and three-quarters of the developing markets' merchandise exports are now manufactured products, many of which are headed for America, Europe and Japan to be branded (and usually marketed back to them).

It is the poorest countries, of course, which do least well out of the global system: as the World Trade Organization reported in 2000:

> the decline in the Least Developed Countries' overall share of world trade is a reflection of the fact that the trade of LDCs over the period 1980–97 was susceptible to contractions that were on average stronger than global contractions, while upswings in the trade of LDCs were on average far less pronounced in comparison with global upswings, or even trends among developing countries. This pattern can be explained to an extent by the fact that the structure of exports of many LDCs remains dominated by primary commodities, which in all but a handful of LDCs account for 80 per cent or more of total merchandise exports. At the same time manufactures have been the fastest growing component of world trade, while commodity prices have exhibited a significant degree of volatility.[9]

The pattern which begins to emerge is one of transition, and – in a limited sense – of convergence: the developing markets moving into manufacturing finished products as the richest countries move out and up into the 'higher' stratum of adding intangible value to these products. (In the USA, service industries now represent 60 per cent of GNP and 80 per cent of jobs.) As the middle-income nations increase their wealth through manufactures, so, naturally, the least developed countries take over their previous role as suppliers of raw materials. The LDCs inherit the tiny margins and desperate volatility of this market, and bear the full brunt of globalization's most malignant side. Their position in the system is not unlike that of a medieval serf, who is obliged to spend so much of his time and efforts producing goods for a distant landlord, that he can hardly provide for himself and his family.

One must assume that as the developing countries begin to take on some of the 'value-adding' processes which until now have been the exclusive province of the industrialized nations, the same process of graduation will continue, and companies in the 'second world' will outsource some of *their* manufacturing needs to the least developed countries. In many cases, this is already happening: in the textile industry, for example, labour shortages and rising costs of labour have forced even the leading Asian producing and exporting countries, such as India and South Korea, to move their production facilities to lower-cost countries (Bangladesh, Cambodia, Lesotho, Madagascar or Nepal), as well as to offshore processing zones in China; or in the bicycle industry, the main Taiwanese companies now do most of their manufacturing in China. The result is that the major world exporters are also becoming major importers, buying intermediate inputs to produce the products in which they specialize.

The primary commodities which, presumably, will always be required, will continue to be mined and harvested where they naturally lie or where they can be grown most efficiently, in rich countries and poor alike. It would be nice to think that at some future time, as production and value-adding processes spread gradually downwards in the value chain, no single country will remain entirely dependent on the export of such goods.

It was the Japanese economist, Akamatsu, who elaborated the famous 'flying geese' analogy: nations move in the same direction but at different distances from the leader; labour-intensive industries with simple technology become unprofitable as the extra value-added from those industries cause wages to rise and they are passed on to the 'goose' next in line.[10]

Yet it's difficult, sometimes, not to be struck by the futility of this global model, even if it does (just about) work: the machine runs, but where is it taking us? If its only purpose is to create ever greater surpluses of consumer goods for the lucky minority which can afford them, there is little to recommend it – even for the lucky minority. The entire world is manning a vast and complex production-line, creating endless supplies of ever more unnecessary merchandise for people whose every want is abundantly satisfied – people, for the most part, working in service businesses in rich countries, who spend most of their waking hours marketing these products to people just like themselves, so that they can earn just enough money to go out and consume them at the weekends.

If the system merely wasted time and kept everybody busy, it would be mad but harmless – I am sometimes tempted to say that any system which keeps us too busy to make trouble and helps us to while away the time as we await extinction is no bad thing – but unfortunately the process creates waste in the form of pollution: from the mining and harvesting of the raw materials, to the freighting of products from manufacturer to consumer over increasingly vast distances, to the excess of packaging which helps one product stand out from its otherwise identical competitors, the machine is gradually laying waste to the planet which houses it.

What we desperately need is some tweak to the mechanism of the capital-producing machine which would enable at least part of this vast expense of energy to be usefully transferred to where it is most needed. At the moment, it is a grossly inefficient machine, producing massive amounts of waste products which are simply discarded.

If more of the wealth it produces could simply be fed back into the humbler parts of the machine, it would stand a far better chance of continuing to run for a few more centuries, rather than crash to a halt in a few years because of its uncontrollable waste or, perhaps, a revolution spurred on by its injustice.

The link between economic development and ecological sustainability is of vital relevance to the arguments in this book, and I will touch on it in Chapter 6.

The risky business of being a supplier nation

Being a tiny cog inside this machine is no place for a country with any self-respect. As I mentioned in the last chapter, being a supplier of raw materials, partly finished and unbranded manufactures is a risky business these days. One of the effects of globalization is that producers of consumer goods in the rich world now source their supplies and labour from an increasingly wide range of poorer countries, with increasing ease and flexibility.

The trend towards e-procurement – where producers and purchasers can negotiate supply deals in an online environment – is an additional factor in making the global market for trading raw materials and components increasingly volatile.

In some respects, these trading hubs could be good news for the small producers in poorer countries, as they enable such firms to bid for contracts with large companies halfway across the world – something which they were unable to do beforehand. The barriers to entry are relatively low, as the organizers of these trading hubs are generally keen to offer the buyers as wide a choice of seller as possible.

But the reality is that they are far more likely to benefit the companies with enough money, clout and IT knowledge to make their own businesses compatible with their clients' purchasing portals, and so graduate to the privileged status of 'preferred suppliers.' Companies without this kind of expertise might find themselves more comprehensively excluded from the potential to do business than they would have done before the trading hubs existed.

As IBM say in a recent white paper on e-procurement,

in today's business world, enterprises must be prepared to compete supply chain-versus-supply chain. A company that does not aggressively streamline its relationships with its vendor base will soon find itself at a competitive disadvantage. Going forward, e-procurement will prove to be one of the key strategic differen-tiators that can continue to grow earnings.[11]

That 'aggressive streamlining of the relationship with the vendor base' has a particularly ominous ring for the small supplier in a developing market.

Reverse auctions are an even more merciless and efficient embodiment of the e-procurement model. In a reverse auction, suppliers bid against each other for offering their wares to a manufacturer, and of course bid prices are constantly brought down. Reverse auctions are now consid-ered an important part of e-procurement: as more and more companies try it out, the concept is increasingly finding acceptance as a mode of procurement. The potential for savings are huge, as 70 per cent or 80 per cent of a company's turnover is typically spent in procuring goods. In India, for example, the pharmaceutical giant SmithKline Beecham (now Glaxo SmithKline) realized savings of 17–20 per cent through reverse auctions for sourcing some direct materials.[12]

E-procurement isn't yet very big: by 2004, B2B e-commerce as a whole is predicted to represent just 7 per cent of the $104 trillion in global sales transactions – but the attractions to the purchaser are such that it seems likely the upward trend will continue. As IBM note:

> Consultants estimate – and our experience supports – that by committing to an aggressive deployment of an e-procurement solution, a company can expect to save between five and fifteen percent of their total procurement spending and to begin seeing results in 6 to 9 months.

It's hard to believe that companies will remain indifferent to such an attractive proposition for very long.

The word 'aggressive' crops up again and again in the literature of e-commerce, and there is certainly something merciless in the way that such instruments force prices ever downwards. Some would claim that this is par for the course in business, and the only alternative is protectionism for certain countries and certain companies against the forces of competition, which are fair and natural, if harsh: and protectionism, the same people would claim, is both undemocratic and unfair. If you don't like the heat, some would say, get out of the kitchen.

The trouble is, not everybody has anywhere else to go.

An absolute faith in the fairness and justice of the savage rules of competition and free-market enterprise may be well-founded in the context of the individual, closed Western economies where it was first observed; where every enterprise starts with essentially the same advantages, and where failure does not usually equal starvation. But an increasingly unified global economic system is a different matter entirely: the extremes of success and failure are greatly amplified, and the borderline between what is harsh but fair and what is utterly brutal becomes increasingly hazy.

Profiles of emerging market economies

The economic profiles of an emerging country and a developed country differ widely, and not just because the numbers are followed by very different quantities of zeroes: characteristically, the revenues of developed countries are much more evenly distributed over a wider range of exports – some commodities, some finished goods, some branded, some not. The emerging markets will usually show a much more limited range of exports, almost exclusively unbranded, and often a significant dependence on one product or group of products. Anyone who has ever tried to run a business knows that excessive dependence on a single source of income is a worrying sign: should that source falter or fail, the consequences can be catastrophic.

It's exceptionally rare for a developed country to depend on a single export for more than a few percentage points of its foreign revenues: Japan and Germany suffer from relatively high exposure in that nearly 12 per cent of their total foreign income comes from sales of cars, but this risk is in both cases spread across several very powerful and well-respected global brands. No single product category of the USA, the UK, Italy, France or the Netherlands accounts for more than 8 per cent of the country's total foreign income.

The picture is very different in developing markets: to give a few examples at random, Estonia derived nearly a quarter of its foreign income in 2001 from the export of telecommunications equipment; a third of Kenya's export income came from tea; copper and copper ore account for 40 per cent of Chile's overseas sales, and 44 per cent of Ecuador's revenues were from the sale of crude oil and derivatives. But even these worryingly high figures are nothing compared to the dependence of some of the very poorest countries on single sources of foreign revenue: take Nigeria, for example, whose exports of oil, gas and other fossil fuels represent 99.6 *per cent* of its foreign earnings.

All of these exports are unbranded products, and leaving aside the case of Estonia, are also commodities, so their sale is primarily influenced by price. Even the highly-finished telecommunications products manufactured in Estonia turn out to be a pretty fragile line of business – especially when you consider that almost all of this foreign income derives from the exports of one company, Elcoteq, a Finnish-owned electronic components manufacturer which built a factory in

Estonia in 1992 in order to take advantage of cheap semi-skilled labour and low property prices.

Elcoteq is itself heavily exposed: until recently, 92 per cent of its sales were to just two companies, Ericsson in Sweden and Nokia in Finland. The fragility of such a business hardly needs emphasizing: in 2001, following a sudden slowdown in the worldwide mobile phone market, Ericsson pulled out of the handset business and sold off its manufacturing plants to one of Elcoteq's competitors. Elcoteq's shares lost half their value in one day and the Estonian subsidiary had to lay off nearly a third of its staff.

As a result of one Swedish brand-owner taking its business away from one Finnish manufacturer with one Estonian factory, Estonia has seen nearly 25 per cent wiped off the value of its entire national exports.

Needless to add, these events barely registered in the Swedish and Finnish economies. Ericsson merged its handset business with Sony of Japan, and the joint venture sold 6.8 m phones and generated sales of $0.9 billion in its first quarter (although, to be fair, Ericsson did make its first-ever loss – over $2 billion – in 2001). Elcoteq also posted a loss but has subsequently built several new factories in China, where labour costs are even lower than in Estonia, and is working hard to replace the lost business from Ericsson.

Wal-Mart and Ugandan coffee

For third-world countries supplying primary commodities to rich companies, the risk of excessive exposure to a single client is even greater.

A convincing case has been proposed for the entire economic boom of the 1990's having been kicked off by Wal-Mart's decision to invest in automated supply management systems,[13] and according to Paul Weatherly, a Washington-based consultant, Wal-Mart's next major impact on the world's economic systems could well be to bankrupt the Ugandan coffee industry.[14]

In the Summer of 2001, Wal-Mart began to sell 100 per cent Brazilian sourced coffee in its North American stores.[15] Most coffee companies use a supply chain of many steps, from the farmer through one or more stages of processing to an exporter, a broker, a roaster, a wholesaler, and finally a retailer. Instead, Wal-Mart has put in place integrated arrangements with Brazilian and Colombian companies that completely bypass the traditional supply chain. One of these companies is Original, in Brazil: because Original grows, processes, roasts, and packs ground coffee in retail tins and ships them from Brazil directly to individual Wal-Mart stores, the Wal-Mart–Original partnership is able to make a profit at a retail price that is 30 per cent to 40 per cent cheaper than the competition.

Directly supplied coffee will end the present market for Ugandan robusta coffee. The coffee sold by Folgers and Maxwell House blends arabica with robusta beans from several sources including Uganda. If Wal-Mart is able to undersell them, Maxwell House and Folgers will suffer a depleted market share or be forced to follow suit. As the grocery industry leader in the US, Wal-Mart is poised to increase its current $560 million in coffee sales as it builds around 3,000 new 'Neighbourhood Markets' over the next 5–10 years (these smaller stores are designed to target the sizeable chunk of the US population Wal-Mart currently misses with its suburban Supercenters).

Wal-Mart has even worse news for Ugandan robusta farmers. Thanks to its highly integrated partnerships, Wal-Mart can sell its own brand of 100 per cent arabica coffee at prices which are 10–15 per cent lower than the 60 per cent arabica/40 per cent robusta blends sold by Folgers and Maxwell House. These products represent one of the principal markets for Ugandan robusta, so if Wal-Mart's customers 'trade up' to the 100 per cent arabica option, as seems likely, then the robusta market will shrink even further.

Wal-Mart's growth in coffee sales is not expected to come from new coffee drinkers – coffee consumption worldwide has been stagnant for a number of years and is unlikely to increase. Wal-Mart's growth will come from existing customers switching from other brands, thus putting further pressure on companies like Maxwell House and Folgers to imitate Wal-Mart's sourcing strategy.

The factors that Wal-Mart looks for do not exist anywhere in Uganda; no Ugandan farmers can provide the kind of one-stop solution which Original gives Wal-Mart in Brazil. But any company wanting to compete with Wal-Mart in the large scale, vertically integrated robusta business needs to consider Vietnam. Vietnam offers favourable factors of production, including modern coffee production infrastructure and ports. When the supermarket brands look for production partners for robusta they will look to Vietnam and Brazil, and possibly Indonesia. Because the market for robusta is likely to shrink as a result of customers preferring the increasingly affordable 100 per cent arabica product, brands are unlikely to consider any other sources.

Seven years ago Vietnam produced less robusta coffee than Uganda but now produces more than five times as much: in fact, according to the International Coffee Organization, Vietnam now produces more coffee than all African producers combined. With such a large single source of robusta that represents no more than 25 per cent to 40 per cent of a mass-market blend, a customer need not look to another source for its robusta than Vietnam or Brazil. There is no reason why anyone would consider Uganda as a source of robusta after Wal-Mart's strategy becomes the industry norm.

Agricultural products supply nearly all of Uganda's foreign exchange earnings, with coffee alone (of which Uganda is Africa's leading producer) accounting for about 21 per cent of the country's exports in 2001; robusta coffee makes up some 90 per cent–95 per cent of this figure.

In a world where, as it is frequently remarked, the biggest corporations are wealthier and more powerful than many countries, it is truly alarming to see how dependent some countries have become on the continued patronage of such corporations. It isn't too hard to envisage a situation where, as a result of one large Western company going out of business or simply deciding to change its supplier, an entire country could be bankrupted.

The case of Brazil

It will take much time, effort, investment and imagination for a country like Uganda to reduce its dependence on agricultural commodities. But some developing countries which inhabit the 'supplier' tier, like Estonia, are patently capable of occupying a higher and less vulnerable position in the global supply chain than they currently do, and are among the first of the developing nations to produce their own international brands. In fact, one Estonian company, Viisnurk, which produces cross-country skiing equipment, has already been doing so for a number of years and currently sells its products in fifteen countries. Remarkably, the company has cornered about 25 per cent of the world market in this highly specialised area.

Ian Batey, in a recent book,[16] has made a prediction that Thailand could produce three new global brands per year; India and China are certainly in a similar position. One country which as yet produces no well-known international brands at all, yet seems abundantly able to do so, is Brazil.

Brazil is something of a puzzle from the branding point of view. It is a rich and powerful nation – at the time of writing, the world's eighth largest economy, and defined by the World Bank as an upper-middle income country (although Brazil is also classed as 'severely indebted', and its wealth is very unevenly distributed: as much as one-third of the population lives in poverty). Yet most of Brazil's foreign income still derives from the sale of raw commodities (such as soya beans, tobacco, iron ore, fruit and coffee), semi-processed goods (such as cellulose, steel, soya oil and sugar) and unbranded manufactured goods (such as shoes, orange juice, sheet steel and automobile tyres). Many of these exports contribute directly or indirectly to the depletion of the country's natural resources. Brazil's foreign income is thus considerably lower than it could be, and is dependent on the increasingly unpredictable vacillations of global commodity markets.

It seems clear that if these low-margin exports were to be enhanced by the sale of branded goods directly to overseas consumers, the level of profit generated by these brands might usefully supplement the income created by the export of commodities and unbranded manufactures: but Brazilian companies, on the whole, don't do it.

Yet it's not as if the Brazilians don't know how to do branding: as the Interbrand survey which I quoted in Chapter 1 shows, branded goods within the domestic market generate billions of dollars' worth of added value to their owners. Brazil has one of the most lively and creative advertising industries in the world, which competes on equal terms with the best of the West: at the international advertising festival at Cannes, the ad industry's annual creative awards, Brazilian campaigns have won more awards (from an international jury) during the last five years than any other country in the world apart from the acknowledged leaders in creativity, the UK and the USA. Many domestic brands in Brazil are rightly renowned for their sophistication. A television commercial for Parmalat (an Italian brand) created by a Brazilian agency was once voted in a nationwide survey as one of the *ten best things* ever to happen in Brazil.

Yet when it comes to exporting, Brazilian products almost never appear under their own brand names, and the country falls into a classic developing market behaviour pattern. The real profits on the export of their orange juice go to companies in America like Tropicana and Minute Maid[17]; the rubber profits go to companies like Goodyear and Michelin; the coffee profits go to companies like Nestlé and Danone; the shoes are rebranded by American and European companies too.

All other factors would appear to be in place: a government which actively encourages export, corporations with the financial muscle to fund international marketing campaigns, plenty of companies manufacturing high-quality products: and yet there's hardly a single Brazilian-owned brand to be found outside Brazil. Even the image of the country from the point of view of overseas consumers is a very positive one – a subject which I will discuss in more detail in Chapter 5.

Somehow, one can't quite imagine rich consumers in developed countries demanding products from Estonia with the same passionate interest that they show in Brazil; and yet, as Viisnurk proves, at least one company is determined to show that their products are worth owning.

Japan, Korea and Taiwan: Asian brand champions

In contrast to Brazil, there are other countries which have consciously pursued a path of export-led economic development, and among their most visible achievements has been their ability to build global brands.

The most striking examples since the Second World War have certainly been Japan, South Korea and Taiwan: Japan went from a nation shattered by war to the per-capita richest OECD member in less than fifty years; the Republic of Korea had the same GNP as Cameroon – indeed, was substantially worse off than North Korea – in the 1960's, yet is now the United States' eighth-largest trading partner and the 11th-largest economy in the world. Taiwan was an underdeveloped, agricultural island fifty years ago, and is now America's seventh-largest trading partner and eighth-largest export market; it is a creditor economy, holding one of the world's largest foreign exchange reserves of more than $100 billion in 1999. Between the three countries, tens of millions of people have been lifted out of poverty, and it is hard to reconcile these facts with the view that international trade does not help growth and growth does not help the poor.

Not coincidentally, all three countries produce world-beating brand names in valuable and profitable product sectors, notably consumer electronics, information technology and motor vehicles.

None of this has happened by accident. Economists often assume that such miracles are primarily the results of free trade, whereas developmental capitalists put it down to industrial policy and system-atic state intervention to support growing industries. In these cases, it would appear to be the latter rather than the former: all three countries have followed a policy of first excluding foreign imports in the market sectors which they have earmarked for development, then copying and improving on the foreign products, and then doing every-thing possible to encourage the export of branded domestic products.

The copying of Western products as a springboard to developing domestic expertise was a fundamental aspect of these countries' road to prosperity: it is said that in the 1950's, the Japanese actually renamed a small island 'Sweden', so that they could legally claim that their matches were 'made in Sweden'. And, as a good illustration of how China is currently following in the footsteps of Japan, I have in front of me a bronze and black torch battery which looks exactly like a Duracell, but on closer inspection is called 'Guanglihua'. Where the Duracell battery says 'EXTRA HEAVY DUTY,' this one says 'EXERY NEAVY DUTY' (an easy enough mistake to make when you're trying to copy words in an unfamiliar alphabet); and most amusingly, the use-ful little chemical strip which, on the Duracell, tells you whether the battery has any charge left in it, is simply printed as a flat image onto the side of the Guanglihua battery, and serves no purpose whatsoever. It's an interesting parable of brand value: there's a big difference between purely cosmetic branding and real added value.

But as I have mentioned, companies in poorer countries can often obtain a faster and more effective apprenticeship through the practice of Western brand-owners outsourcing their manufacturing facilities.

Incidentally, it's interesting how many of the brand-producing coun-tries are actually quite small (e.g. Taiwan, Britain, Japan, South Korea), and there is no question that small size can prove to be a stimulant in the long run: because they have to export in order to grow and have to brand in order to compete with bigger companies from bigger countries. There is a corresponding advantage for companies in big domestic markets (China, America): you can build 'brand mass' in a safe and leisurely fashion before attacking the world.

But whatever the natural advantages which these 'tiger' economies may have enjoyed, there is no question that it has almost always happened as a result of a deliberate and centrally planned development strategy. Moreover, the critical role which branded exports play in the process has usually been fully understood and entirely explicit.

In 2002, for example, in an attempt to cash in on the publicity that would be generated by the co-hosting of the World Cup soccer finals by Korea, the Ministry of Commerce, Industry and Energy announced an ambitious plan to raise the international recognition – and thereby boost the exports – of Korean brand-name products.

According to a report released by the Ministry, the government's goal is to have Korean brand-name products account for 70 per cent of the nation's total exports and to have at least 10 brand names be included among the world's 100 most recognizable brand names by 2010. And lest anyone doubt that the initiative has the necessary backing, the plan was unveiled at the 2nd Industrial Design Promotion Meet, attended by government officials including Prime Minister Lee Han-dong and around 200 industry representatives.

To achieve the goals of the project, the government has worked out five strategies: to internationalise Korean brand-names, strengthen corporate brand management, reinforce electronic brand marketing, expand the infrastructure for brand marketing; and raise the nation's image abroad.

The government has announced that it will create a 100 billion won venture fund to help exporters improve the designs of their products. The ministry will also open 'industrial design renovation centres' in 10 cities nationwide to help small and medium-sized companies improve the design of their products as part of an integrated effort to boost the value and recognition of Korean brands.

In 2002, the government chose 300 brand-name products that are internationally competitive in terms of technology and design to develop them as leading Korean brands. The government's plan to build up the nation's 'brand infrastructure' includes the opening of a 'Brand Academy' to train about 500 specialists every year in brand management, character design and industrial packaging.

In Japan, Taiwan and South Korea, it has always been seen as a primary duty of the bureaucracy to 'pick winners' – strengthening companies in specialized markets by providing capital and export incentives, and to 'keep a pristine home base' – closing domestic markets to strong overseas competitors while domestic favourites captured market share at home and abroad. In other words, the bureaucracy was founded upon mercantilist principles, and its primary function was to produce growth.[18]

All of this sounds heavy-handed to say the least, and it has always been one of the conclusions of the argument for 'infant industry protection' that free trade does not necessarily produce optimal levels of growth. But the alternative to protectionism is simply to rely on the shock therapy of instant liberalization, and hope that in the face of sudden exposure to the full force of globalization, a kind of natural selection will produce robust, world-class brands. In many cases, this is simply too unequal a contest, and will result in an unacceptable waste of promising companies which, in time, could have developed into valuable exporters. The 'international community' must simply accept – in deeds as well as words – that a degree of temporary preferential treatment is necessary if emerging economies are to stand a chance of becoming valuable trading partners in the future.

As Tina Rosenberg points out in a recent article,[19] 'the argument that open economies help the poor rests to a large extent on the evidence that closed economies do not'.

The basic conditions which are necessary in order to give rise to the kind of development which we have witnessed in the more successful Asian economies are essentially those which Adam Smith summarized as 'peace, good government and the regular collection of taxes', but the English economist, Ronald Dore, gives a fuller account:

> a strong central government whose strength lies in the quality of political leaders and administrators, more concerned with promoting the national interest than with feathering their own nests through the corrupt use of power; a high savings rate; substantial investment in education, health and the physical infrastructure for industry and trade; a supply of intelligent and resourceful entrepreneurs, more interested in building something lasting than in gambling on movements in market prices. The trajectory has also involved, at least until a quite advanced stage of development, controls over external trade, and even stronger controls over capital movements in and out of the country – even in countries such as Taiwan and South Korea, hailed during the Cold War as models of free enterprise development.[20]

Sautter more succinctly describes Japan as a 'pro' state: in other words, one that is successively or simultaneously producer, protector, prospector and programmer[21]: the same could be said of South Korea and Taiwan, and the conclusion is irresistible that, to some degree, this style of governance is probably an essential part of kick-starting a growth export economy.

These are valuable examples for emerging countries to observe, and there is a great deal which a benign and brand-friendly government can do (even within the strictures of WTO regulations) to ensure that promising companies and high-potential brands are encouraged, nurtured and stimulated.

The role of government in encouraging and promoting branded exports is an issue to which I will return in Chapter 5.

How the instinct to brand has become global

Mainly as a result of the power and ubiquity of the big global brands produced by the most successful brand-producing nations (in Interbrand's top 100 global brands, 61 are American, 8 are German, 6 are Japanese and 6 are British), brands are a noticeable feature in the lives and landscapes of the vast majority of the world's population today. From hoardings, packaging, television and cinema, magazines and newspapers, websites, floor-stickers, shelf-tags, tee shirts, petrol pumps, the backs of bus and cinema tickets and the lids of takeaway food containers, brands target the world's population with a constant monologue from which it is almost impossible to escape. These brands are like tiny economic portals, sucking in money and sending it down the pipe to their parent companies.

Even in Cuba in 1987, a visiting American professor reported landing behind the iron curtain in Havana, but instead of the statues of Lenin he expected to see, there was 'the biggest Visa Card that I had ever seen, above the words, "Welcome to Cuba."'

The following year, the same intrepid traveller hiked deep into the highlands of Guatemala, and found that 'half a day's walk beyond the last electric wires, in "guerrilla" territory, beyond the reach of government, Coca-Cola and Pepsi were still slugging it out, with Coke reigning supreme. Malnourished campesinos would spend a day's wages for a warm bottle of Coke, el sabor de la vida Norte Americano.'[22]

But the effect of all this isn't merely that consumers are encouraged to be more brand-aware and perhaps to buy more products: anybody who produces anything is also stimulated to experiment with the same techniques, and aspires to the same levels of potency and ubiquity. The instinct to brand is becoming more and more commonplace. Awareness and adoption of marketing practices has itself become globalized, as Kent Wertime notes in a new book[23]:

> Globally, brand management is a relatively consistent practice . . . consequently, the integrated marketing tactics that made Michael Jordan or Pokémon famous are replicated almost anywhere you go. Local Canto-pop singers, for example, endorse everything from fizzy drinks to furniture stores. Indian cricket stars help hawk

tea and skillets. Dragon boat races in Hong Kong and beach volleyball tournaments in Rio attract corporate sponsors and a raft of merchandise that follows. The local media pump out a stream of commercial messages in fairly similar formats around the world. The marketing mechanisms tend to be the same.

One of the consequences of the absolute ubiquity of brands and branding is that no manufacturer anywhere in the world really needs to be introduced to the idea of brand equity: it is all around us, and must, during the last few decades, have worked itself into every producer's consciousness as the ultimate commercial aim, the target towards which all entrepreneurial ambition inevitably tends.

This is surely one of the reasons why the phenomenon of emerging brands from developing markets is beginning to gather pace.

So where are the brands?

It would seem that, apart from the interesting exceptions, some of which I will discuss in Chapter 3, most emerging countries remain firmly in the supply business, and scarcely ever venture into branded exports.

In Western countries, the creation of international brands has normally followed as a consequence of the first appearance of domestic brands; and domestic brands first appear in any given country when certain conditions are in place – economic development, market sophistication, consumer demand, competition, trademark protection, media choice, the right retail conditions and so forth.

Once domestic brands have been around for a certain length of time, some of the owners of these brands may begin to consider marketing them overseas. This might be as a result of increasing competition at home, a general increase in the size, ambitions and prosperity of the companies, suitable export market opportunities in the form of overseas colonies, or free-trade agreements with other countries, and so forth. Often, there will be a history and a habit of trade with other countries, and the notion of exporting a branded product comes as a logical consequence of this. Sometimes, an opportunity to export a brand occurs when an overseas market is at an earlier stage of development in the process of consumerization: in other words, there is less competition, and the sophistication of the imported brand means that it can make a killing there.

Many middle-income markets are at present somewhere between the two stages of producing domestic brands and producing export brands. In most developing countries, local as well as foreign brands have been part of the landscape for many years – more recently in the case of ex-communist countries, but in several emerging Asian and Latin American countries, domestic brands have been around for decades. But these brands have seldom, if ever, ventured out of the domestic marketplace, apart from the occasional 'downhill' export to poorer countries, where such brands are considered aspirational and desirable.

Often there have been no branded exports because it is usually finished goods which are branded, and in many cases the only finished goods exported from emerging markets have been commissioned for manufacture there by brand-owners in industrialized nations.

Brands – both domestic and international – have almost always appeared in the past as a *consequence* of certain levels of market sophistication and economic and social development. But even though this has usually been the typical pattern, it is feasible to fast-track the creation of export brands, and if this is done successfully, a wide range of benefits can accrue both to the company and to its home country or region as a whole.

I would argue that the development of international brands is, in today's globalized world, as inevitable and essential for the growth of an individual economy as the development of domestic brands has been in the past: for many countries, this kind of development simply can't happen too soon.

It is said that American brands have an advantage on the global market because they have first been developed in one of the toughest domestic markets on earth. In fact, the experience of having to hold one's own in a developing country under the onslaught of highly-sophisticated and massively funded European, Japanese and American brands is probably just as tough a test.

In cases where, as I described earlier, there is no significant protectionism in an emerging market, local brands are obliged to do battle with global brands in a more or less Darwinian scenario. The presence of imported brands tends to accelerate the 'progress' of market sophistication, as it heats up the competitive environment, stimulates the domestically-produced brands – the ones which they don't buy up or put out of business, that is – into greater sophistication (local brands can sometimes prevail simply by being more finely attuned to the cultural characteristics of consumers than the global brands, or by eliciting a sense of loyalty or heritage in the consumer). At the same time, consumers in emerging markets are also exposed via the international media channels to a great deal of popular culture which arrives more or less unaltered from the wealthy countries for which it was originally produced, so they are already attuned to the style and sophistication of western communications.

So, one way and another, the progress from basic marketing to sophisticated brand communications tends to be fast-tracked in developing countries. (This is very much in the interest of global brand-owners, incidentally, since it enables them to use regional and even global advertising campaigns in all of their international markets, which creates major savings for them).

What it also does is to provide an accelerated learning-process for domestic manufacturers. The ones which survive quickly learn how to do their own branding, and, in time, they may well be able to start selling their own brands abroad – at first in less developed markets than their own, because 'downhill export' is the route of least resistance – but perhaps eventually in the home countries of the multinational companies whose brands threaten their existence.

I believe that the transition from unbranded to branded goods, and from branded domestic products to branded exports, has the potential to be far more than just the symptom of economic development: that brands, perhaps uniquely among all the other factors of development, have the unique ability to 'drag along' many of the other factors if they are deliberately pushed to the fore of commercial development.

'Brand Leap'

Having strong and well-known export brands enables both companies and countries to punch above their weight.

The point about brands is that their area of influence is in perception, and this perception works in many directions: not only does it add appeal to the product for the consumer, it also brings confidence to the producer and improves the reputation of the industry and the country which makes it. The addition of attractive and powerful brand equities to well-made products can fast-track the acceptance and success of those products in international markets, and increase the speed of development and progress in their country of origin in various unexpected ways. In this respect, brands are as much cause as effect, and the overall picture is of a virtuous circle.

The pride which countries take in their own brands of international renown underlines this point. The birth of Red Stripe Beer, for example, Jamaica's principal export brand, was considered a milestone in Jamaican history. When the island gained independence from Britain in 1962, a columnist for the *Daily Gleaner* wrote: 'the real date of independence should have been 1928, when we established our self respect and self confidence through the production of a beer far beyond the capacity of mere Colonial dependants'.

A beer brand as a symbol of a colony's independence may sound a little far-fetched, but similar sentiments are expressed wherever a smaller or poorer country produces an internationally-celebrated brand: the fact that consumers halfway across the world, perhaps richer, perhaps poorer, are happy to spend their hard-earned money on *our* product, is a powerful token of enterprise, of commercial prowess, of a tiny but real influence over the daily lives of ordinary people the world over.

Brands are also linked to innovation, which is in turn linked to greater profitability. I mentioned in the first Chapter that a brand is as much an open invitation to complain as it is a guarantee of quality; in a similar way, it is also a constant inducement and obligation on the part of the brand-owner to practise continuous innovation.

'Invisible' companies can continue to produce 'invisible' products and nobody much notices if, year after year, they do pretty much exactly the same thing. But branded products and services have deliberately placed themselves in the limelight, and this creates a high level of expectations which the brand must satisfy if it is to keep purchasers loyal and interested.

In a less pronounced way, the same is equally true of countries: once a country becomes known as an exporter of quality branded goods in certain product sectors, overseas consumers will have higher expectations of that country as a source of products, and to some degree will be looking out for a steady stream of new exports from it.

According to the PIMS study which I mentioned in Chapter 1, branded businesses are more than twice as likely to undertake significant innovation. Again, whether this is cause or effect is impossible to determine, and probably immaterial: the fact is that the companies which succeed tend to be those which want to succeed, and the desire for success is characterised by an above-average investment of time, money and energy into improving products and building reputation. Better products build a strong reputation, and a strong reputation creates the need for better products.

The 'limelight' effect on a company of brand-building has an effect on employees and managers which is just as potent as its effect on consumers: even production line workers can feel a degree of pride in knowing that they are contributing to the creation of a product which is famous (as long as they have no other reason to dislike their employer, of course). It is easier to create a sense of team spirit, so vital for productivity and quality, when the end result of everybody's co-operation is a respected household name. It is easier to recruit and retain good employees (again, all other conditions being equal) if a company produces well-known products.

All these reasons are a powerful argument for companies having a brand strategy right from the start: a sense of what their brand stands for (and external brand image should be and usually is closely connected with the ambitions and 'vision' of the company), where it is heading, who it is targeted at, and what it offers them in addition to the basic functional attributes of the product. The earlier such a brand-oriented approach is introduced into a company, especially if it is targeting overseas markets, the greater the benefits that will accrue.

And as the Red Stripe example shows, the same arguments apply equally to countries.

Success for a country or for a business has many components – management, quality control, financials, employee relations, recruitment, market position and innovation – and building a powerful and trusted brand is just one of these. However, the order in which these components are developed, emphasized and invested in can be varied to some degree, and with differing effects. Some are chronologically fixed – for example, you can't hope to build a powerful brand without first developing rigorous quality control – but others are variable, and the importance they play in the growth strategy of the organization usually depends on the management and strategic style of the owners and managers.

Until the second half of the twentieth century, brand-building was seldom an issue which companies consciously considered in their early days, nor was it a quality which companies believed it was possible to control: rather, the assumption (which experience bore out) was that through decades of offering consistently high quality to consumers, loyalty was built, and a good reputation – a strong brand – was the consequence. Certainly, this 'organic' approach to brand-building, where the company's brand values grow up purely spontaneously, built by consumers with very little conscious help from the company, does create very robust brand values, but it takes a very long time. It also depends on a marketplace where products can differentiate themselves entirely on functional superiority to their competitors for long enough for their brand values to accrue.

Obviously, times have changed, and companies now need to think about the reputation they want to build and the image they want to create from the moment they begin to conceive and design their products: because their brand values will quickly become their primary or unique competitive advantage.

For all these reasons, taking an early and proactive approach to brand development has a unique power to accelerate the growth of companies and their countries of origin. In 'natural' circumstances, as I have said, brands tend to emerge as a consequence of certain other factors being in place, but if their emergence is deliberately brought forward in the lifecycle of companies – and especially in clusters of exporting companies from a particular country – they have a unique power to 'pull forward' the other conditions of growth.

Brands can perform their own version of 'technology leap'. In just the same way as mobile telephony, for example, has achieved widespread growth in several emerging countries before fixed telephony ever had a chance to achieve any kind of coverage or quality, so *brand leap* can enable companies in emerging countries to graduate to exporting branded products before passing through the usual preliminary stages of unbranded domestic production, branded domestic production and unbranded export. In the next chapter, there are several examples of companies in poorer countries which have done precisely this.

In conclusion:

1. Branding, once the brand is established, should create an increase in profitability and customer acquisition and retention, so there's every reason to kick-start it early in the process – as long as the products are good enough to sustain the brand promise, of course.
2. Branding creates highly visible success stories which encourage other companies to follow suit, more enthusiastically and faster than they otherwise would. Brands are the rock-stars of commerce, and create many fans, both at home and abroad.
3. Branding creates expectations of product quality which the manufacturer has to work twice as hard to maintain: this accelerates the development of a first world-style approach to both quality control and innovation. Putting your own brand name on your products 'raises the bar'.
4. Examples of single companies in the West tend to show that the companies which understand the importance of brand early on in their growth – and practise it well, and build their corporate strategy around it – are often the ones which grow fastest.
5. Having a powerful brand – even if it is merely in strategic form, without solid customer recognition yet behind it – makes companies more powerful. They are perceived by investors, competitors, suppliers and other businesses as more valuable, and carry more weight in all kinds of negotiations. Potential value, if it is clearly reasoned and intelligently planned, is universally recognised as real value; strategy, creativity and ambition are universally recognised as indicators of potential.

For producers in poorer countries, it is very much in their interest to do battle in the area of intangible values, because this is the area where their natural advantages are strongest: a compelling and unusual brand story, an unexpected or unfamiliar country of origin, a different and exotic 'brand culture' and imagery – in short, a real point of difference.

Competing primarily in the area of functional attributes rather than brand values compels companies from emerging markets to do what they have almost always done in the past: to leverage low price, their only other asset. But as we have seen, low pricing is an unsustainable if not suicidal strategy for poorer countries in a globalized world, and it diminishes rather than enhances the reputation of both company and country of origin. Instead of going forwards, discount-based exporting makes companies and countries go backwards.

Clearly, the challenge for government is in ensuring that the growth of the company benefits the country or region as a whole, but to a degree it's inevitable as long as there's enough of it. As I showed in

Chapter 1, even absolutely selfish company owners can't achieve growth without spreading some of their profits into the immediate environment: growth means they need to spend more on supplies, services and taxes, to build buildings, to hire workers and managers.

As long as the necessary obligations are placed (and enforced) on companies to respect minimum wages, supplier credit terms, building regulations and environmental legislation, to pay their taxes and report their earnings, then the success of the business will unfailingly be shared to some extent. The extent may be relatively small, but this simply means that it's doubly in the interest of governments to ensure that as many companies as possible are motivated and incentivized to follow suit. The 'brand effect' will achieve much of this on its own.

I have mentioned the other conditions of growth, such as innovation, creativity and quality in this chapter, but haven't dwelled on them in any great detail, because the importance of brand is the primary focus of my argument. However, all these attributes are closely linked with each other, and it is worth stressing the importance of quality, in particular, as the primary requirement and basic precursor of all other factors in the equation, including brand. I mentioned that branding is futile, if not impossible, unless the quality of the product is unimpeachable, and it's worth pausing for a moment to consider where this quality originates from.

At the heart and origin of many successful companies is a story of one person's obsession with creating a high-quality product or service. A high proportion of such companies are started by a *product man* or *product woman*: somebody whose primary interest in life – if not their sole interest – has nothing to do with consumers, or money, or success, or even ordinary ambition: just a single-minded, almost unhinged commitment to *making the best product*. Without this, there can be no brand.

These rather rare people, as we shall see later, are the entrepreneurs who need to be spotted, educated, funded, praised, encouraged, nurtured and treasured by their home towns and home countries if they are to flourish and bring fame and wealth back home.

Such natural talent is always in rather short supply, and it mustn't be wasted. Because of its rarity and oddity, it often goes unrecognized, and it is seldom compatible with mainstream educational performance. Care must be taken to ensure that when schools and colleges eventually kick out the students who simply won't fit in, won't go by the rules, and are driven by curious obsessions which have nothing to do with the school curriculum, they aren't kicking out the very men and women who might one day make a sizeable contribution to their country's future prosperity.

If you govern a country which needs to grow, it's worth considering this point, and understanding that these men and women are your future. Treat them well, and the investment might be repaid many, many times over.

CHAPTER 3

Developing markets, emerging brands

Deepak Kanegaonkar

Deepak Kanegaonkar has been Managing Director of his company, Vishudda Rasayanee (Pvt) Ltd., since he founded it in 1990. The company, based in the Indian city of Mumbai, manufactures glycol ethers, polyglycols, brake fluids, coolants, phenoxyethanol and oil field chemicals.

And, rather unexpectedly, it also makes two world class, premium grade luxury perfumes, Urvâshi and Lata. But you won't yet find either of these perfumes in your nearest airport duty-free shop: Urvâshi is only sold in a few select Paris department stores – it's not available in India at all – and it currently retails for around 130 euros, in a handcrafted silver flacon made in Rajasthan. Urvâshi is described as 'a combination of the creamy scent of sandal with the soft aroma of mogra flowers, and is evocative of all the sensuality and mystery of eternal India'. Lata, named in honour of the legendary singer Lata Mangeshkar, is only available in India, and features jasmine, rose, sandal, musk, vanilla, amber, oakmoss and patchouli. It is currently the most expensive perfume in India.

The perfume side of Deepak's business, Gandh Sugandh, is only a few years old, and after he made the momentous decision to expand from industrial chemicals in 1997, Deepak had great difficulty persuading people that anybody was going to buy his perfume, especially in Paris, the world capital of fine fragrances. The first formulations of Urvâshi were not liked by consumers in European tests – in fact, one or two people in the Swiss research groups commented that the perfume had a 'doggy' smell.

But after many more tries, far too lengthy to recount here, Deepak finally got it right. The vital ingredient of Urvâshi is pure *chandan*, or sandalwood oil, from Karnataka. This precious substance is strictly controlled by the Indian government, and cannot be used by any other perfumier, but its scent is noticeably superior to the synthetic analogues used in other perfumes. Deepak had to fight hard for an export licence to get it out of the country, and fight twice as hard again for an import licence to get the finished product into France, where perfume in a silver container had not been imported since legislation began, and no product category existed to calculate the correct tariff. In the end, an eighteenth-century category relating to the products of 'perfumiers and silversmiths' was resurrected for his benefit.

The brand name, Urvâshi, comes from Hindi mythology: Urvâshi was an *apsara*, one of the beautiful immortal maidens who live in Paradise and entertain the demigods with their singing and dancing. Urvâshi was created by the sage, Narnarayan, to be the most beautiful of heaven's creatures. But she became bored with heaven and, on one of her many night-time excursions to Earth, fell in love with a mortal, Pururava, and on meeting him again – after many travails – in the garden of Gandhmadan (a word which means 'intoxicating fragrance'), they were finally married.

If it is true that brands are enhanced by their stories and by their cultural richness – a point which I will discuss again in Chapter 5 – then Urvâshi surely has a rather special potential.

At every stage of his new enterprise, Deepak met with scepticism and resistance, both at home and abroad. Almost nobody believed that it was possible for an Indian company to sell perfume in France. The Indian ambassador in Paris, Kanwal Sibal, voiced the opinion that Deepak's venture 'was like making F-16s in India and trying to sell them in the US.' (To his credit, he changed his mind after meeting Deepak, and ended up hosting the launch party for Urvâshi in his Paris residence).

And perhaps it's not too hard to understand why people sneered at the idea. For nearly a century, perfumes have been almost exclusively sold under the brand names of the great French and Italian fashion houses – Yves Saint Laurent, Chanel, Givenchy, Dior, Guerlain, Fendi, Versace, Gucci, Armani – and it's exceedingly difficult for any other brands to break into this highly profitable but highly brand-conscious market, unless it's in the wake of successful clothing sales.

Ironically, these houses have often looked towards the East for their inspiration: many bestsellers like Yves Saint Laurent's *Opium*, Guerlain's *Shalimar* and *Samsara*, Boucheron's *Jaipur* and Chopard's *Mirabai*, base their brands and their marketing on Asian imagery of one kind or another.

Take, for example, the way Guerlain describe *Samsara:*

> In Sanskrit, Samsara means the eternal cycle of life. It is an imaginary place, sacred and mysterious, where Orient and Occident meet. Samsara is the symbol of harmony, of absolute osmosis between a woman and her perfume. It is a spiritual voyage leading to serenity and inner contemplation.
>
> The bottle, in the sacred red of the Orient, echoes the figure of a Khmer dancer in the Musée Guimet in Paris, her hands folded in a gesture of offering, expressing plenitude and femininity. The stopper evokes the eye of Buddha, a symbol of meditation which leads to detachment and supreme enlightenment.

Yet the launch of Deepak's *Eau d'Urvâshi* is almost the first time that a branded perfume has been able to murmur this kind of nonsense with any conviction, because it really comes from the place it claims to come from.

In fact, there was nothing terribly new about what Deepak was attempting to do: the art of blending fragrances originated in the East more than four thousand years ago, and sandalwood had been used as an essence for over two thousand. Attars, bath oils, flowers and incense were an integral part of an Islamic lifestyle that further enriched India's cultural mosaic, not only in visual aesthetics but in sensuality, too. The *Kama Sutra* recommended the use of perfumes made with camphor, sandalwood, jasmine and rosewater to create the right ambience for love-making. Even the Prophet Mohammed is said to have remarked that the things he loved most in the world were 'women, children and perfumes'. Scented incense continues to be an integral part of rituals in most traditional Indian homes. Oriental cuisine is suffused with aromatic spices like cardamom, cloves, cinnamon and saffron. The Song of Solomon in the Bible is a virtual treatise on aromatic herbs, spices and scents, both native and imported from the East. Islamic expertise in trade helped eastern aromas – perfume oils, precious herbs and spices – waft freely to the western world.

But when, after a gap of many centuries, an Indian presumes to resume this ancient but broken tradition, the Paris couturiers mutter that no third-world upstart can possibly claim to understand the art and magic of perfume – not to mention the art and magic of brand management – as they do.

This view is, apparently, not shared by the well-to-do shoppers of Paris, who are splashing on *Eau d'Urvâshi* as fast as Deepak can ship it to them.

Perhaps the cleverest thing which Deepak did was to spend a significant proportion of his limited budget on hiring a French marketing expert – Anne Faure-Sailly, previously European Managing Director for Calvin Klein perfumes. Deepak persuaded Anne to work for him by the simple but charming expedient of inviting her to Mumbai for the public launch of Lata, and then (in front of the assembled Indian press and television, 200 photographers and some 2,000 guests), introducing her as his new European General Manager. Anne, unable either to confirm or deny the surprising announcement in such company, saw Deepak the following day at a press conference in his apartment, where he begged her to accept the job, announcing that he had already booked three million French Francs' worth of advertising space in Vogue and Marie-Claire for the French launch of Urvâshi.

To her credit, and with some courage, she accepted, and was rewarded by the disconcerting but touching experience of having her feet embraced in the taxi by Deepak's wife on the way back to the airport.

Faure-Sailly used every ounce of her considerable influence and credibility with the French perfume industry, the distributors and the retailers, to get a small stock of Urvâshi into a couple of Paris department stores just in time for Christmas. The product was shipped way behind schedule and had to be flown in from India at vast expense. Despite the poor quality plastic gift packaging and almost no publicity, the product sold out in days.

The same thing happened the following Christmas, and 800 gift boxes of Urvâshi were sold out in two weeks – this time with an elegant new cardboard wraparound, designed by Anne, doing its best to disguise the cheap plastic gift-box (Deepak had been talked into buying five years' supply of the boxes by the manufacturer). Anne also included a newly-designed stopper for the flacon, laid it on a little silk cushion in the box, a ribbon, and packaging in saffron-yellow (representing the sun) and red (representing the spirit of welcome), based on a mosaic design from Rajasthan. This year, Chanel began to develop its own rather similar plastic gift box, a sure sign that the newcomer was attracting attention.

But profitability for Anne and Deepak was still a distant dream, not least because the product simply cost too much to produce – the silver for the flacons, for example, needed to be imported from Switzerland to Rajasthan, because the local silver wasn't of the right quality to hold perfume. Deepak invited the two leading French perfume bottle companies to propose designs for a new glass flacon, and, unable to say no to either of them, accepted both designs. Deepak's resources began to run out, and in 1999 his chemicals company was finally bankrupted by the cost of running Gandh Sugandh, the perfume business.

At the time of writing, the company is urgently seeking new backers.

In an interview with an Indian newspaper just before he launched Urvâshi in Paris, Deepak was asked what was his aim in undertaking this extraordinary venture. His answer was simply: 'to make India proud'.

Kamthorn and Panudda Kamthornthip

Kamthorn and Panudda Kamthornthip, the proprietors of the Cha-Lom Co. Ltd., founded their company in 1990, the same year as Deepak started his business, but three thousand kilometres away in Bangkok.

Their stories are not so very different. Until the moment Deepak decided to create his own brand, he was an anonymous manufacturer for other companies, enduring the tight margins which that kind of business implies.

The Kamthornthips also had a margin problem: their company, a garment manufacturing business, was making children's clothes for American brands like Guess, DKNY Kids and Osh Kosh. They had invested heavily in quality control and new manufacturing technology in order to win these accounts (when the company started, their biggest clients were the local Bangkok department stores), and recently had been awarded a major accolade when Baby Guess and Guess Kids Asia started entrusting the company with both the design and production of children's clothes.

The company was doing well, but the cost of wages in Thailand continued to rise, and like many other Thai manufacturers, Cha-Lom was constantly at risk of losing business to factories in Indonesia, Vietnam, India and Bangladesh. Many other Thai garment manufacturers responded by relocating their manufacturing to areas like Kanchanaburi, close to the Burmese border, where uncontrolled immigration means that labour costs can be up to 20 per cent cheaper than in Bangkok.

But Kamthorn and Panudda realised that competing on price alone was a dead-end strategy: and one day, just like Deepak, they decided that they would like to see a name of their own creation on the labels of the garments their workers were making.

So they invented BeBe-Bushh. Not, you might think, a brand-name which trips lightly off the tongue, but then English is not the Kamthornthips' native tongue, nor is the Roman alphabet their alphabet, so a word which ended with the letter 'h' twice probably didn't strike them as being particularly unusual.

Now, you could, if you wanted, go to one of the specialist American or British brand-naming consultancies and pay them a great deal of money to tell you that a name which ends with two aitches and sounds like a cuddly toy representing an American president is neither memorable, spellable, pronounceable or likely to succeed on the international market. And you'd be as wrong to spend all that money as they would to tell you so: because a name like BeBe-Bushh is *so* odd as to be quite remarkable. Make no mistake: this is a brand which, once you've figured it out, you will never forget.

'Convincing people that Thailand is a place that can produce stylish and internationally competitive brand-name clothes was not easy,' says

Panudda Kamthornthip. This is probably the understatement of the century; but as she points out, 'the first step was specializing our expertise in children's clothes and improving our production enough to take orders from famous foreign design houses'. The point is an important one: Western companies' habit of manufacturing in poorer countries can – quite unintentionally – provide their suppliers with an invaluable leg-up onto the branding ladder, and might unwittingly be laying the foundations for a new generation of competitors for the hearts and wallets of their consumers.

BeBe-Bushh children's clothing is now sold in around a dozen countries, from Japan to America, alongside Osh Kosh (another name which the consultants would probably advise you against using) and DKNY Kids, and sells for a similar price. Kamthorn's business now operates at a margin which is many, many times greater than it was when his garments were sold with somebody else's label on them. Many of Cha-Lom's clothes are sold in stores that carry only the company's brand, including 50 shops in Germany and eight in Dubai.

Those Thai companies which do not improve their quality or begin establishing brand names will simply not survive, according to Chavalit Nimla-or, president of the Thai Garment Manufacturers Association, in an interview with the *International Herald Tribune* in 2000.[24]

'Companies that try to compete on price alone will soon die,' says Nimla-or. 'Thailand's garment industry will only survive by upgrading.'

As the *Herald Tribune* article notes, the garment trade, one of the country's largest industrial employers and its second-largest exporter after makers of computer equipment, has considerable importance in the Thai economy. One wonders what kind of a seismic shift in confidence will be required before a statistically significant section of the industry decides to follow where Panudda and Kamthorn Kamthornthip are leading. One thing is certain: without leaders, there can be no followers.

Like Urvâshi, in its own modest way, Cha-Lom carries a little local culture with it when it travels abroad. The *cha-lom* is a traditional Thai shopping basket, woven from bamboo strips. When the cha-lom is full, the bamboo strips that are left undone are tied up with apiece of string. Although tourists can still buy a cha-lom in souvenir shops, the object is now rarely used in everyday life – but perhaps in a small way, the Kamthornthips' brand is helping to keep the memory of this old tradition alive.

Roustam Tariko

A new brand of vodka from Russia might not sound like a particularly original or surprising idea: after all, the one kind of brand which consumers in the West will happily purchase, and pay a premium for, is a food or drink brand which confirms that what you're buying really does come from the country most famous for producing it.

So, in the same way that nobody would quibble about buying Italian rather than Bolivian pasta, or feta cheese from Greece rather than from Lithuania, or Tokaï from Hungary rather than Wales, most people think it's perfectly natural to choose a Russian vodka brand.

But how about a Russian brand of *banking*?

Roustam Tariko, just like Deepak and the Kamthornthips, woke up one morning with a vision. In his case, it happened in around 1997: this young Tatarstan-born entrepreneur had originally created a niche for himself helping Italian businessmen find hotel accommodation in Soviet Moscow in the early days of *perestroika*; the niche became a highly profitable business when he became Martini & Rossi's first-ever Russian distributor. Within six years, Tariko had become the biggest Martini importer in the world, and by 1998 he was ready to produce his own brand.

Russki Standard is a super-premium vodka which retails in the US, Italy, UK, Greece, Hungary, Bulgaria and the Baltic Republics for at least 10 per cent more than the premium Swedish brand and market leader, Absolut. Russki Standard is the only vodka which is still distilled to the tsar's premium quality standard established in 1894, and enjoys a 60 per cent market share for all premium vodka brands, both imported and domestic, at home in Russia.

Today, Roustam's group of companies controls over 80 per cent of the sales of all premium alcohol in Russia and is a long-standing exclusive distributor of such brands as Martini, Smirnoff, Bacardi, Johnnie Walker, Gordon's, Bailey's, Metaxa, Di Saronno, Veuve Clicquot, Jägermeister and others.

Most interestingly, the group also includes a successful and fast-growing retail bank, Russki Standard Bank, and Roustam sometimes talks about expanding the bank abroad.

As a branding idea, it is, to say the least, somewhat counter-intuitive: in fact, a Russian bank is about as unconventional as a Russian vodka is conventional, and about as alarming as a Russian vodka is reassuring. But who knows how consumers in other countries might respond to such a quirky offering (assuming, of course, that sufficient reassurances could be given of the bank's probity, resources and stability)? After all, who could have predicted that we would queue up to buy boots and shoes from Caterpillar, a maker of bulldozers, or airline tickets, vodka, mobile phones, investment plans and wedding dresses from Virgin, a record label?

And if you ask Roustam what is his motivation in introducing Russian brands to the world, his answer sounds like something Deepak might have said:

> I'll strive to make the brand that will be recognised by the world as a symbol of Russia. It would be one of the happiest days of my life if someone came to me and said, 'Your brand helps us to understand Russia.'[25]

David Tang

One of the best-known examples of an emerging global brand which comes from and is manufactured in an emerging market, and derives much of its imagery from its country of origin, is Shanghai Tang, the fashion brand created in 1994 by Hong Kong businessman, David Tang Wing-Cheung.

A natural salesman and a well-known figure on the London party scene, Tang describes his brand as 'the best of 5,000 years of Chinese tradition exploding into the 21st Century'.

Tang's privileged background – an expensive English education and an upbringing in one of Hong Kong's wealthiest families – has certainly not stilted his ambitions, which occasionally over-reach themselves: the highly-publicized 1997 opening of a flagship store in New York's Fifth Avenue (where the rental was probably in excess of two million dollars per year) was swiftly followed by a rather low-key relocation to cheaper premises in Madison Avenue. But the brand continues to prosper in other prestigious locations, such as the Peninsula Hotel and the airport in Hong Kong, Ngee Ann City in Singapore and Sloane Street in London. Each store opening is a high society event in itself, attended by a carefully-invited bevy of supermodels, journalists and minor celebrities. And, of course, that's the way the fashion business works.

Tang's glamorous tale is certainly very different from the titanic struggles of entrepreneurs like Kanegaonkar, the Kamthornthips and Tariko to escape the obscurity of small business life in emerging markets, but it is part of the same process: people taking pride in their home country as well as their products, and refusing to accept that their only hope is in competing for the privilege of manufacturing anonymously for one of the great global brands.

Jiří Kejval

Jiří Kejval, aged just 35, is the founder and chairman of Techo office furniture, based in the Czech Republic. The company's head office is in Prague, and has branches in Bulgaria, Hungary, Poland, Romania, Slovakia and London. Techo is a good example of a successful business-to-business manufacturer which is just beginning to develop into an international brand.

Jiří tells in an interview in the *Prague Tribune* how one of the first lessons he learned about export marketing was quality control: in 1992, his company was making floodlights and received a major order from IKEA, the Swedish furniture retailer.

> They returned the order to us due to poor quality. So we did it over, and they returned it again. Finally, the third time, they

accepted it. We were financially exhausted, but it taught us to shift to Western quality standards.

Techo's export strategy also shows the wisdom of starting by exporting 'downhill' in order to build the experience and bulk necessary to attack 'uphill' markets. By the late 1990's, the firm was already the outright leader in the Czech market, but as Kejval says, 'there's nothing worse than being number one on a market and waiting to see what the competition will do'. Their first overseas venture was in Romania; by 1998, its sales had already reached 1.5 million dollars. This was followed by a fast-growing Hungarian branch and a meteoric entry into Poland, which was later cut back due to recession. Techo had also had a Slovak branch since Partition in 1993. Finally, in 1999, Techo UK opened in London, and its struggle uphill began.

Just like Deepak Kanegaonkar, Kejval made the very sensible decision to invest in a local expert, so they hired an experienced British furniture merchant, Barry Folley, who founded the branch almost single-handedly. Techo UK's revenues rose to CZK 87 million (nearly 3 million euros) just a year after its founding, and its first customers included the London branch of Accenture, the Royal Air Force, The Financial Times and even Buckingham Palace.

Having moved rapidly from unbranded to branded domestic manufacturing, and then from branded domestic sales to branded export sales, and from downhill to uphill export marketing, the firm's next move is to raise the barriers to competition and enrich their brand through expertise rather than simply rely on high-quality design and manufacturing. In the end, a great product can always be copied, and small firms doing well are particularly vulnerable as they start to attract the attention of larger companies, which, with their larger resources, can easily outdo them in price, quality, speed to market and brand values – or buy them out. So Kejval's strategy is to start to embody the acquired experience of the firm into its offering, and rather than simply sell furniture to companies, advise them on how best to design and fit out their offices in order to achieve maximum productivity, staff satisfaction and welfare, customer appeal and loyalty. 'We don't sell furniture, we sell office solutions,' he says.

Finally, and most interestingly, Techo is a firm which understands the value of culture in building a rich, complex, attractive and inimitable brand.

It was a relatively small step from commissioning original design for its products to actively supporting art, and as Kejval says, 'Techo's management is well aware of the danger of unification and the importance of distinguishing its production from that of its competitors'. Techo soon became known not only as a furniture maker but also as a publisher of limited edition books and an organizer of graphics exhibitions. In 2000 Techo published an edition of Franz Kafka's 'I Enter a Room and I See . . .' a publication which subsequently received first prize for illustrations in the national contest for 'Most Beautiful Book of the Year'. Even the firm's own brochures, Techo Horizont and Techo IQ, took third place in the Catalogues category, the best placing ever achieved by any commercial publication.

'Techo is one of the few domestic firms that dared connect itself with art,' says Jaroš Milan, one of the firm's graphic designers. 'The firm gives me a free hand in creating the catalogue, which cultivates both customers and the firm itself,' he says. As Techo's PR coordinator Kateřina Čapounová notes: 'a Techo sales representative won't bring you a pen or a plastic bag with the firm's logo, he will bring a book. This makes a completely different impression'.

This is a wonderful example of a fundamental principle for brands from emerging markets: positively connecting your brand with the culture of your country of origin provides an *almost ineradicable competitive advantage*. No matter how big or powerful or competent Techo's Western European and American competitors may be, the one thing they can't be is Czech. Turn Czech-ness into a competitive advantage in the eyes of your consumers, and you have created a barrier to imitation which the others simply cannot overcome.

Automotive

Once you start looking for emerging international brands from unexpected places, it's astonishing how many you can find. During the research for this book, I have found nearly two hundred brand exporters in the second and third worlds whose story is worth telling, and I get the feeling I'm only scratching the surface. For the sake of brevity and readability, I won't attempt to cover them all, but many are worth a brief mention.

In the field of motor vehicles, it is particularly hard for smaller countries to remain competitive, as the capital costs are so high. For a small company, it's next to impossible to match the ability of the big American and European manufacturers to pour hundreds of millions of dollars into design, research and development and marketing, and yet still have the scale to produce budget models at accessible prices.

Nonetheless, despite the stony ground, there are companies here and there which have managed to find a niche. Some produce highly specialized vehicles, like **Adria** of Slovenia, a company which makes campers, mobile homes and motor caravans which are sold in Austria, Belgium, Denmark, Finland, Sweden, France, Spain, Italy, the Netherlands, Switzerland, Ireland, Yugoslavia, Croatia, Macedonia, Germany, Poland, Portugal, Slovakia, Britain and even Japan.

Other companies which, like Adria, design and manufacture bodies which are twinned with larger companies' engines and chassis, include

Marcopolo of Brazil, a builder of bus bodies, a business in which Brazilian firms are becoming world leaders: Brazil produces 15 000 buses per year or 10 per cent of worldwide production, and it's one of the country's very few named exports, even if the name is always subsidiary to the brand of the completed vehicle.

South Korea is the only developing market with a volume car man-ufacturing industry and several global brands (**Hyundai, Daewoo, Kia, Ssangyong**), but Malaysia's **Proton** is making some progress in the same direction. Some of the auto manufacturers in ex-Communist countries still produce cars, generally at low prices for the domestic market and near neighbours; several of these have been taken over or invested in by European manufacturers, like **Dacia** of Romania, bought by Renault, **Škoda** of the Czech Republic, bought by Volkswagen, **Zastava** (makers of the **Yugo**), which has had support throughout its history from various Western companies, including Chrysler in the 1930s and Fiat from the 1960s. Now the Serbian-owned corporation is trying to recover after its factories (which also manufactured arms) were bombed by NATO during the Balkan conflict in 1999, and is build-ing cars again, this time with Peugeot engines and Porsche-designed transmissions.

The **Lada**, a Russian-built car, has also enjoyed some popularity abroad during its long life, and like the Yugo, this has mainly been because of its exceptionally low price. Today, the company still pro-duces three different front-wheel-drive models, and has, to date, built over 20 million cars. Lada still exports about 100 000 cars annually.

Škoda is perhaps one of the best examples of how strong negative perceptions of an emerging-market brand can be harnessed by the right marketing approach to create major shifts in attitude: of all the ex-Soviet cars, only the Škoda has succeeded in shaking off the expec-tation of cheapness. In 2000, 60 per cent of the UK population stated that they wouldn't consider buying a Škoda (a car which like many ex-Communist products, was the butt of popular jokes). Eighteen months later, this figure had fallen to 42 per cent, and sales increased by 23 per cent, thanks to the combination of a greatly improved and more attractive product and a humorous advertising campaign which directly confronted people's negative perceptions of the product. This change in perceptions has undoubtedly also had an effect on the aver-age British consumer's perceptions of the Czech Republic too.

There are a number of semi-independent car, truck, bus and motor-cycle companies active in India: the most successful of these, **Maruti**, has benefited from its long-term partnership with **Suzuki** of Japan. Maruti has a strong international presence with sales in over 70 coun-tries: in some like Malta, Sri Lanka, Nigeria and Sudan, the vehicles are sold under the Maruti brand name, and the company has positioned its recent model, the Zen, as a 'world car'. Until India opened its markets to the outside world, the most popular car, indeed practically the only car available, was the **Ambassador**, manufactured by Hindustan Motors, and the car is still something of a legend – although not properly speaking a viable brand, since you can't buy it outside India – around the world.

The biggest independent player in India is **Tata Engineering**, the automotive division of the Tata group, one of the country's largest private sector companies. It is also India's leading commercial vehicle manufacturer. Tata cars and SUV's are exported to the Middle East, Asia, Africa, Australia, Latin America and Europe. Out of total revenues of nearly US $2 billion, around $150 million derives from export sales.

Mahindra off-road vehicles are also to be found in South America, the Middle East and Africa.

The Society of Indian Auto Manufacturers lists several smaller companies which manufacture scooters, mopeds and motorbikes, including **Premier, Bajaj, TVS, Majestic** and **Maharashtra**, but of these only **Royal Enfield** has a recognized brand outside the domestic market.

Royal Enfield's story is a fascinating one. The first Enfield motor bicycle was manufactured in England in 1901, and nearly fifty years later, two young Indian businessmen, Mr. Sundaram and Mr. Shankar of the Madras Motor company, started importing the Bullet motorcycle into Madras. In 1955, they set up the first Enfield India plant, which really marked the beginning of the era of motorcycling in India. At first, Enfield Bullets were sent out to India in kit form and assembled there, but before long, the entire bike was manufactured in India.

Fifteen years later, in 1970, Royal Enfield UK finally went out of business, unable to compete with the better made, more attractive and cheaper Japanese bikes which were flooding the British marketplace. But the Indian operation survived and prospered – mainly because the Indian market was still closed to foreign imports and escaped the onslaught of the Japanese newcomers.

Today, Royal Enfield has a network of 13 marketing offices and 223 dealers in all the major cities and towns of India, 25 spare parts distributors and stockists, and 150 Authorized Service Centres; it exports motorcycles to over 30 countries including the USA, Japan and Germany through five international offices, 25 importers and over 200 dealers around the world. This world-beating Indian export is especially popular in the United Kingdom: a brand-new classic British bike, made in India, at a fraction of the cost of a Japanese bike.

Many automobile tyre brands have been developed in the poor countries which produce the rubber from which they are made, and although the global brands are mainly European and American (Pirelli, Michelin, Goodyear, Dunlop), there are examples of emerging markets which are beginning to build international brands, such as **Kumho** and **Hankook** tyres of South Korea (Hankook is currently the world's 11th largest tyre manufacturer and aims to be the fifth largest by 2007), **Lassa** of Turkey (the sixth largest producer in Europe), and even some from the rubber-producing countries themselves, such as **Gaja Tunggal** tyres of Indonesia, which are exported throughout the Asia-Pacific region.

Food and drink

There is a particularly rich seam of global brands from emerging markets to be found in the **food and drink** sectors. This isn't altogether surprising, as travellers have always enjoyed bringing home exotic food and drink from distant countries – it's a way of experiencing a place when you can't be there in person or remembering it if you can't go back. But food and drink are low-ticket items, and you need to distribute and sell in pretty large quantities in order to achieve meaningful returns.

The international food brands produced in developing countries are often condiments of various kinds – **Lee Kum Kee** of China, **Pic-a-Peppa** sauce from Jamaica, **Ukuva Zulu Fire Sauce** from South Africa, **Vegeta** seasoning mix from Croatia (which is sold in forty countries), to name but a few – and some companies, like the Satnam Overseas Group of India, have done good business overseas by selling domestic produce to their diaspora. Satnam's leading brand of basmati rice, **Kohinoor**, is available in stores in the US, Canada, the UK, Europe, Africa, Australia and throughout the Middle East where rice is a staple but not locally produced; until recently, the brand was only available in traditional Indian stores but it is beginning to make an appearance in the major multiples, and thanks to the growing acceptance of Indian cooking alongside Italian, French, Chinese, Mexican and Japanese as a true 'world cuisine', Basmati is beginning to become a common purchase well beyond the Indian diaspora. Satnam has another 12 brands behind Kohinoor: **Super Kohinoor, Rose, Three Horses, Shahenshah, Charminar, Trophy, Falcon** and the oddly-named **Football**.

Perhaps the most unexpected country of origin in this category is Fiji: **FMF Biscuits** has succeeded in establishing export markets in the USA, Australia, New Zealand and Pacific Island countries for its range of crackers and cookies.

And it's worth remembering that Japan's **Kikkoman** soy sauce was already exported worldwide long before Japan had begun to emerge as an economic force; **Amoy** soy sauce was also known around the world when the original company moved from Xiamen in China to Hong Kong in 1928. The company has been wholly owned by the Danone group since 1991.

Amoy is also one of a small number of companies which have even succeeded, or are beginning to succeed in establishing restaurant chains in developed countries – others include **Nando's** of South Africa, a fried chicken chain, and **Jollibee** of the Philippines, a fast-food outlet which is outdoing even McDonalds in its home market – mainly as a result of catering more competently to local tastes. With over 400 outlets in the Philippines, Jollibee has also opened stores (designed primarily for Filipino expatriates but also frequented by locals) in Hong Kong and the United States. And the Cuban government-owned operator of Cuba's Pizza Novas, in conjunction with the government-owned Gran Caribe hotel chain, is currently planning to open Cuban cuisine restaurants in Brazil, China, France, Italy, Mexico and Spain, where a licensed, branded **Cuban Tropicana** nightclub has existed since 1994.

And yet food – of the unbranded sort – is the poor world's primary export to the rich world, so the lack of branding in this category is all the more noticeable. A key reason is simply that poor countries generally export produce in bulk and unprocessed form, whereas the branding of food usually occurs after the processing stage – the famous name being added after the food has been cooked or prepared in some way, and is owned by the importer, the packager, the distributor or the retailer.

Some brands also prove that it is possible, although tricky, to brand agricultural produce: the earliest examples of global produce brands from emerging markets were probably **Jaffa** from Israel and **Cape** and **Outspan** from South Africa. Many countries have found that it is very hard to maintain any kind of market position in foodstuffs unless some kind of brand equity can be built up around the country of origin – hence the attempt to brand New Zealand kiwi-fruit as **Zespri**, for example. The advantage to the consumer represented by the brand name can be based on packaging, convenience, distribution, freshness, quality control, seasonality, or more emotional associations – perhaps simply that a given country is just the 'right place' for a particular product to come from, although experience suggests such positionings don't tend to survive a more convenient, more easily available, or more attractively priced alternative, even if it does come from the 'wrong' country (which is why consumers in the UK buy more mozzarella cheese from Denmark than Italy).

Seasonality is one of the trickiest factors when dealing with produce, as it's one of the aspects of production which is beyond the producer's control. But there are ways around the problem: for example, it would be perfectly possible for two developing countries in different climate zones to develop a co-branding strategy, where each fills the gaps in the other's growing season, and between the two, a range of branded products could be supplied all year round. Perhaps the twinning could even be between one emerging country and one developed country, as a 'partnership programme' for development purposes. The 'brand story' of a cold country and a hot country working together might be rather an original one too, with its own unique appeal to consumers. Even those consumers who complain about the year-round availability of produce in the West destroying the sense of changing seasons in our diet, might find some romance in the idea of the brand switching from 'hot' to 'cold' halfway through the year, and back again: from Zespri Sun (produced in Sri Lanka) to Zespri Snow (produced in New Zealand), for example.

Working in a rather different way are the various **FairTrade** products, and other poor-country produce marketed under similar schemes, usually run in wealthy countries with the specific intention of helping producers in poorer countries to get a fairer price for their produce on the international market. I'll talk about these in more detail in Chapter 6; they have a special importance to the debate as they have, or aim to have, a direct impact on the fortunes of some of the very poorest countries.

Beverages: a cornucopia of global brands

The **beverages** category is enormous, and contains more global brands from emerging markets than any other – and what is particularly noticeable is how many countries produce branded and bottled beer for export (over fifty, by my reckoning). An almost random selection of these drinks brands includes: **Angostura Bitters** (Trinidad & Tobago), **Boh** Tea (Malaysia), **Budwar** beer (Czech Republic), **Cobra** beer (now produced in the UK, but originally, like **Kingfisher** beer, an Indian-brewed product: sadly, the company's founder, Karan Bilimoria, could only get the quality he wanted from UK brewers), **Director's Special Whisky** (this brand made by the Shaw Wallace company of India is the fastest growing liquor brand in the world, recording a growth of 98.2 per cent over the five year period 1993–97), **Concha y Toro** wine (Chile), **Dos Equis, Sol, Tres XXX, Superior** and **Tecate** beers (Mexico), **Egri Bikaver** wine (Hungary), **José Cuervo** tequila (Mexico), **Maraska** plum brandy (Croatia), **Mr Brown** iced coffee (Taiwan – spotted for sale as far afield as Slovenia and Cyprus), **Pilsner Urquell** beer (Czech Republic, now owned by a South African company), **Red Stripe** beer (Jamaica), **San Miguel** beer (Philippines), **Singha** Beer (Thailand), **Sisserou** liqueur (Dominica), **Tiger** beer (Singapore), **Lion** beer (Sri Lanka), **Tsing Tao** beer (China), **Zwack Unicum** digestive (Hungary), and many, many more. **Rotkäppchen** sparkling wine, one of the very few brands produced in Eastern Germany, is doing so well it has recently bought Mumm, a top West German brand, from Britain's Diageo, and is now presumably in a good position to export to other countries, should it wish to do so.

Natural Waters of Viti (Fiji) and **Radenska** (Slovenia), are just two of the many 'national' mineral water brands which do well in distant export markets. Of all the products for which country of origin is critical, mineral water ranks alongside airlines as the one whose brand values are usually most closely associated with those of its provenance; and almost every country in the world has at least one mineral water brand – ranging from one or two (usually state-owned) labels in countries like Oman, Congo and Cuba, through around 140 in Britain and the USA to a staggering 582 in Italy. It's no accident that a huge number of water brands have pseudo-Italian names (in fact the leading water brands in Ecuador, Poland, Denmark, Russia and Azerbaijan are all called *Aqua Minerale*, in only slightly mis-spelled homage to the supremacy of the Italian product). Branded waters tend to identify themselves closely with their country or region of origin because water almost never has any attributes or benefits of its own to distinguish it from its competitors. Wine, whisky and other drinks may always be sold on product attributes – on taste, on quality, on colour, on heritage, on price – but water is an attribute-neutral product as it has none of these distinguishing marks. It is simply a transparent 'front' to the nation brand (and often, within the domestic marketplace, the region brand).

Dilmah Tea, the business of the charismatic Sri Lankan entrepreneur Merrill J. Fernando, is a particularly good example of a developing-market firm which has successfully made the transition from bulk supply to globally branded product. Having worked in a UK tea company Fernando returned to Sri Lanka and joined A F Jones & Co., a British owned and managed tea business. He became its Managing Director within two years and eventually bought out the British shareholders, shortly afterwards supplying the first ever consignment of Ceylon Tea direct to the then USSR. In his twenties, Fernando went on to establish Merrill J. Fernando & Co. Ltd., originally supplying bulk tea to most of the world's major tea brands in the 1960s and 1970s and soon became one of the top 10 tea exporters in Ceylon, and the only Sri Lankan owned one to enjoy this success. In the 1980s, Fernando imported the first teabagging machine into Sri Lanka in spite of discouragement and opposition from the Tea Board and his clients. The machines went underutilized for several years as Merrill faced the wrath of bulk tea customers who believed that Sri Lanka should remain a raw material supply source and Europe, USA, Australia and New Zealand the value addition points. Fernando's vision was based not on the politics of development but rather on the simple fact that, by supplying consumers direct from origin, the quality and freshness of tea could be improved without additional cost, in every market. Naturally the multinationals thought differently since their interests lay in sourcing product from multiple origins regardless of quality, and branding the commodity in such a way that the country of origin would not be relevant. Dilmah is now exported to 82 countries around the world, and other Sri Lankan tea firms are beginning to follow in Merrill's footsteps.

One of the many hundreds of exported lagers from the Eastern side of Europe, **Laško Pivo** of Slovenia, is worth a special mention. When the beer was first brewed in 1825, Laško, the small town in eastern Slovenia where the brewery still stands, was part of the Austro-Hungarian Empire, and Laško Pivo was exported as far as India and Egypt. Under Socialism, the company managed to retain its traditional quality standards and its domestic consumer base, but lost its international fame. By 1985 it was the leading brand in Slovenia, and had the largest market share of any of the 28 Yugoslav breweries; it had even started to export again, doing some business in neighbouring Italy and Austria. After the disintegration of Yugoslavia, Laško, like so many companies, lost half of its marketplace, but managed to retain some of its scale by exporting to Croatia and Bosnia during the Balkan war. Today, Laško Pivo is by far the leading brand in Slovenia, with a market share of over 50 per cent, and in Bosnia (with a 25 per cent market share). Two years ago, the company acquired a brewery in Split, and thus became the No. 3 brand in the Croatian market too. Exports to Serbia, Kosovo and Macedonia were re-established in 2001, and are growing rapidly.

Besides being an excellent beer with good distribution, the brand's key success factor seems to be its unique image: it is regarded throughout South-Eastern Europe as an imported brand, but not a foreign one like Heineken or Carlsberg. As a Slovene brand, it is politically palatable, and is happily consumed by Serbs, Croats and Muslims alike, who normally avoid each others' brands on principle. Exports to Italy and Austria remain small but stable, mostly in the border regions, but the company is now considering plans to build on its domestic success and enter new markets in Central and Eastern Europe, including the Czech Republic – which would be a move akin to Deepak selling his perfume in Paris[26].

It has almost always been possible for poorer countries to produce global liquor brands: part of the reason is probably just the Westerner's insatiable appetites for travel, alcohol and variety. Exotic tipples have always been seen as trophies of travel, and it's not surprising that quite a few of these brands came to fame in the days of Empire. Nowadays, most of the international alcohol brands are owned, marketed and distributed by a few large conglomerates such as Diageo, Allied Domecq and Pernod-Ricard, even if they are still produced in smaller and sometimes poorer countries. Independently-owned drinks brands don't stand much of a chance of acquiring international distribution unless they belong to one or other of these global brand portfolios, whose enormous size and financial muscle gives them great influence over the distribution and retail channels.

The size to which a successful alcohol brand can grow is remarkable. The only brand to feature in Interbrand's top 100 Global Brands which doesn't come from a major economic power is Bacardi, from

Bermuda – a very small, though rather rich country. Bacardi is the world's 75th most valuable global brand, and with a valuation in excess of $3 billion, is worth comfortably more than the GDP of the country which produces it.

Fashion, footwear and accessories

Some of the better-known brands in this area include **Bata Shoes**, which comes from the Czech Republic (although when then brand was originally established in 1894, Czechoslovakia was decidedly in the first world). Since then, Bata have sold more than 14 billion pairs of shoes, more than the number of pairs of human feet that have ever walked the earth. In addition, there are dozens of fashion brands which sound as if they're Italian or American but are produced and sold somewhere quite different, such as **Bossini** and **Giordano** (Hong Kong), **DiCaprio** (Croatia), **Ragazzi** leather goods (Thailand), **U2** (Thailand), and so on. One of the distinctly American-sounding brands, **Buddy Davis**, which is manufactured by Maral Fashions of India, is sold in Europe as well as in India. From Brazil, **Forum** and **Triton**, the brand creations of a gifted designer, Tufi Duek, are sold throughout Latin America and the USA.

However, one Brazilian clothing brand which is as yet not available outside Brazil under its own name, appears to have enormous potential: **Hering**, a brand of underclothes and possibly the best quality plain white tee-shirt you can buy, is a brand produced by a large textile company and sold very successfully in the domestic market; abroad, Hering's business is limited to supplying unbranded tee-shirts for companies like Walt Disney and Coca-Cola to brand with their own designs and logos. Since the plain white tee-shirt is a staple of many men's and women's wardrobes all over the world, and there is almost no single, dominant brand, the situation is very reminiscent of the market for casual men's trousers until Levi's spotted the gap and launched Dockers.

Hidesign leather bags, briefcases and accessories (from India) are sold around the world, although this is one example of a brand which made the conscious decision to conceal its country of origin: 'We're an international brand with a presence in India as in other countries. I wouldn't want to categorize my brand as Indian. Why does a brand need to come from anywhere?' said Dilip Kapur, the president of Hidesign, in a recent interview in the *Economic Times*. He maintains that the designs do not reflect Indian culture and have 'a very cosmopolitan international travellers' look', and positively recoils at the suggestion that these very high-class products might have some kind of 'ethnic' appeal. And quite right, too: if the target market one is aiming at is the international jet-set – or its modern equivalent – then statelessness is certainly one of their characteristics.

The South African diamond giant **de Beers** is also a global brand from an emerging market, as well as the owner of one of the best-known advertising slogans of all time (*a diamond is forever*), and is useful as an illustration of the feasibility of branding commodities. It is also yet another sad example, along with several of the oil-producing nations, of how a poor country can discover that it is sitting on vast reserves of natural wealth, yet still remain to all intents and purposes a poor country.

Sporting goods

A few exceptionally successful emerging-market brands appear in this category: **Elan** skis from Slovenia supplies between eight and ten per cent of all skis worldwide. Making around 75 per cent of its sales abroad, Elan was a leader of the export-led economic development which laid the foundations for Slovenia's present prosperity in the 1980s. It went bankrupt in 1990, hit by Yugoslavia's economic problems, but as an independent Slovene company is once more on the road to recovery.

Elan is best known for introducing the first 'carving' ski, a technology which was swiftly copied by every other major manufacturer, and which now account for 70 per cent of global ski sales. The company also makes leisure boats, which provides a useful means to offset the seasonality of ski products.

A smaller Slovene company, **Goltes**, is becoming fairly well-known as a manufacturer of snowboards and paragliding products, and is tipped by some to become the next Elan.

Viisnurk, as we saw in Chapter 2, is an Estonian company with a similarly impressive market share in its chosen niche, accounting for something like 25 per cent of the world's production of cross-country skis – around 300 000 pairs per year. These are sold under the brand-name **Visu** in around fifteen countries, and the company has recently made a promising move into hockey sticks, using the brand-name **MaxxHockey**.

Other notable international brands in the sector include **Double Happiness** table-tennis bats and balls from China and **Huğlu** shotguns from Turkey, which have a global reputation for quality. The brand, Huğlu, is actually not the name of a company but of a small town on the pine-covered slopes of the Taurus Mountains in central Turkey. Gun craftsmanship was brought to Huğlu in around 1914 by two master gunsmiths who had learned gun maintenance and repair in the army during the First World War and opened their first workshop there. After a few years, their business became the biggest in town, and other gunsmiths began to open their own workshops nearby. Later, a cooperative was established to improve their production and marketing strategies.

Today, there are more than 100 separate workshops and more than 600 craftsmen employing about 500 additional workers in Huğlu, making around 65 000 shotguns each year.

Bicycles are an important manufacture of emerging markets – principally of China, India, Taiwan and Indonesia – and in a market like China (where there are probably half a billion bicycles on the roads), there is every opportunity for manufacturers to build significant 'brand mass' at home before exporting.

China has around 40 per cent of the world's market for bicycles, but almost none of the brand action. The **Shanghai Bicycle** company of China is a major exporter, although its brand is largely unknown outside the domestic market: almost all Chinese manufacturers remain in the OEM (original equipment manufacturer – i.e. unbranded) business and are re-badged by local or international brands at their destination. However, most major manufacturers have realized that the OEM business leaves them vulnerable to cut-priced competitors in countries where overheads are lower, and are working hard to develop branded products. **Phoenix**, the world's largest state-owned cycle manufacturer, has a somewhat uncertain future following China's entry into the WTO.

Probably the most successful cycle export industry in the developing world is in Taiwan: unlike mainland China, Taiwanese companies don't have a massive domestic market to exploit, so export is a more pressing need, and around a billion euros' worth of finished bicycles were exported from Taiwan last year. It may have been partly this pressure to expand abroad which helped to create Taiwan's **Giant**, the world's leading cycle manufacturer. As the company's blurb states:

> Across seven continents and fifty-odd countries, underneath thirty-two of the world's brightest professional cyclists, in over ten thousand retail outlets, and throughout the streets of the world's most populous nations, you'll find bicycles designed and built by Giant, 'The Global Bicycle Company.'

The Taiwanese cycle industry has not been slow to recognize the need for more companies to follow Giant's illustrious example, and its industry association repeatedly sends out messages like these to its members:

> It is clear that the Taiwan bicycle industry is chiefly export-oriented since the local market is relatively limited, and that it must maintain an international perspective. Domestic makers began with OEM for foreign brands and gradually accumulated the production technology and strengthened their ability to innovate.
>
> In recent years some Taiwan manufacturers have started to place emphasis on promoting their own brands in line with OEM production, and reaching for the high-end bike market. They have also developed several new lead acid/nickel cadmium batteries

for electrical bicycles. Sales outlets in foreign markets are being established and overseas factories are being set up for a market edge with a global division of labour.

Starting off as OEM suppliers, Taiwan's cycle firms must strengthen their brand consciousness if they wish to overcome competition from low-cost manufacturers in China and Eastern Europe. Only successful brands can maximize corporate value and open up long-term niches. Cycle firms should strive for exceptional products, individualized marketing, mastery of logistics, utilization of e-business, and the simultaneous pursuit of global and localized marketing.

Atlas Cycles of India are sold in over forty markets around the world – the EU's savage anti-dumping duty on Chinese bicycles between 1993 and 1998 provided the 'window of opportunity' for companies like Atlas to expand quickly into many overseas markets – but Atlas is an infant in international marketing compared to Giant: as yet, overseas sales contribute a mere 10 per cent to its total turnover. But then, like the Chinese companies, Indian manufacturers have such a huge domestic market to supply, it's not surprising if export sales are something of an afterthought.

Emerging-market bicycle production has proved a major threat to the established companies in the developed world. At first, it was simply the usual story of improving quality and low prices which drove the Chinese, Indian and Taiwanese manufacturers to their current global market share of 40 per cent, putting many European and American producers out of business in the process, including Schwinn/GT, America's largest manufacturer, and Raleigh of Britain. *The Economist* reports that annual American bike production has fallen from 9.9 million units in 1994 to 500 000 in 2002.[27] But, despite import tariffs and anti-dumping duties against Asian products, the growth in market share of Asian producers is relentless, and as time passes it is the brand appeal of companies like Giant which is polishing off what remains of the West's cycle industry. All that is left are a few niche players in specialist sectors such as high-performance racing bikes, where, as with a few other industries dominated by Asian brands, such as cameras and binoculars, a European brand name still carries a certain amount of cachet.

White goods and other consumer durables

China has proved full of nasty surprises for many Western manufacturers: hundreds of billions of dollars have been invested in Chinese ventures, by thousands of foreign firms, since 1992, yet few Western companies have succeeded in making any money in China. Whirlpool, for example, launched enthusiastically in China in 1994, building factories to manufacture the domestic appliances it confidently expected to sell to the Chinese, only to find that it couldn't compete against domestic brands.

After losing more than $100 million and shutting down most of its factories, Whirlpool now manufactures washing-machines for Guangdong Kelon, one of its Chinese competitors, which are sold to Chinese consumers under the **Kelon** brand.

Another of Whirlpool's domestic competitors is **Haier**, which claims 25 per cent of the substantial US market for hotel mini-bar refrigerators, and set up its own manufacturing plant in South Carolina in 1999. Its products are sold in over 160 countries and regions, and more than 38 000 sales outlets have been established across the world. According to the *China Daily*, the Haier Group now has a 5.3 per cent share of the global refrigeration market, ranking second in the world, just one percentage point behind Whirlpool.

Haier is not, however, one of those emerging-market brands which chooses to make its country of origin part of its brand communications – and doubtless its acceptance in the United States and elsewhere is helped by the German-sounding brand name (which is not entirely a fiction – the company was originally known as the Qingdao Refrigerator Plant but renamed itself in honour of the production line technology which it purchased from the German Liberhaier Company some eighteen years ago).

In the *Financial Times* list of the world's most respected business leaders in 2000, Zhang Ruimin, the Chief Executive of Haier, was placed 26th: quite an unusual place for a businessman in a Communist country to find himself.

The *China People's Daily* has a good deal to say about the further prospects of Chinese brands on the world stage, and its report on the proceedings of a recent symposium on the question of branded exports is worth citing in full:

> Domestic brands are becoming strong enough to challenge the world's top 500 on the global stage in three to five years, according to a report by the Beijing Famous-brand Evaluation Co., Ltd.
>
> The report cited FAW (First Automobile Works), Haier (a household appliances brand) and Legend (a computer brand) as possible candidates.
>
> The evaluation company Wednesday released its sixth annual report on the ranking and value of 32 major Chinese brands in 18 industries. Company representatives said they based their judgments on a mix of sales, profitability, comparison with similar products and input in image building.

The report said that Chinese brands are growing rapidly and are likely to catch up with world famous brands in the next half decade. Sales of Chinese brands are on the rise. The first ten most valuable brands, for example, increased 30.9 percent in annual sales on average, said the company.

Chinese Vice Premier Wu Bangguo called on the Chinese nation to make efforts to promote the development of China's brand commodities so as to benefit the world's people.

In his letter to a symposium on 'China's Rising Famous Brand' held in Beijing, Wu said that development of brand commodities concerns China's economic growth and social progress. He said he believes that with joint efforts from various sectors, China's brand commodities will rise in the world and China's economy will see fast growth in the coming century. Cheng Bangzhu, president of the China Quality Control Association, said that brands have become an important guide for customers when they make purchases.

He said that with the deepening of economic reforms and opening up, many enterprises in China are blazing the way and creating famous brand commodities for the international market. Chen said that the core for famous brands is quality, and he urged China's enterprises to enhance quality control in production and improve products with updated technology.

More than 500 scholars, experts, and representatives from China's enterprises with famous brands attended the symposium.

Reading these words, and those of the similar Korean initiative which I quoted in Chapter 2, it is hard not to be reminded of the single-minded, quality-driven, somewhat heavy-handed attitude of the Japanese government towards encouraging branded exports in the early years of that country's economic miracle. One can only conjecture what the global effects might be of a similar rise to prominence of a country with 20 per cent of the world's population – not to mention the effects of it subsequently faltering in the way that Japan has.

Simply consider the prominence today of Japanese brand-names like Toyota, Sony, Honda, Yamaha, Mitsubishi, Kawasaki, Hitachi, Sanyo, Pioneer, Panasonic, Sharp, Nikon, Shiseido, Hello Kitty, Nintendo, Sega, Nissan, Kenzo, Suzuki, and so forth: picture a similar proportion coming from China; bump up the numbers coming from Taiwan and Korea, and you probably have a fairly accurate picture of the global brandscape in eight to ten years' time. One can't help wondering whether there will even be room left in the stores for very many brands produced in Europe, America and Japan.

On a smaller scale, but in the same industry, the Koc group, Turkey's largest conglomerate, exports its refrigerator brand, **Arçelik**, to more than 50 countries, mainly to European Union Countries as well as to developing markets in the Middle East, South Africa, and Central and

Eastern Europe. The company's declared aim is to become one of the top five European white goods producers by 2005. Perhaps, like Haier, the company might find that a change of brand name would be appropriate before tackling the English-speaking markets.

Gorenje household appliances of Slovenia is Europe's eighth-largest producer of white goods, manufacturing 2.1 million appliances last year at its home factory in the small town of Velenje. It exports more than 90 per cent of its output, with almost two-thirds going to the European Union and the remainder to countries in eastern Europe and the former republics of Yugoslavia. Never short on style, the company had its new line of kitchen appliances designed by Paolo Pininfarina, stylist to Italy's Ferrari.

In no particular order, a few other brands in the category are worth mentioning: **Lomo** cameras from Russia, which have become something of a cult in the US and Europe; the **Cybiko** games computer, also originally from Russia, a hybrid portable e-mail and texting handset, personal organizer and wireless duelling games console, which is available worldwide and has literally dozens of fansites devoted to swapping games, tips and chat about the brand.

Pacific Green coconut wood furniture from Fiji is one of several examples of furniture companies in emerging markets which are beginning to establish some brand loyalty among consumers in richer countries. Although furniture is difficult to brand except at the very high end of the market, the competitive imperative to do so remains strong, and is almost universally recognized. To quote just one example, in its annual review of the Taiwanese furniture industry last year, the China External Trade Development Council (CETRA) made the following observation:

> As manufacturers in Taiwan tend to focus on the development of new manufacture techniques, their controls on marketing channels are weaker. Most of the control power inevitably falls into the hand of foreign companies, who thus earn plenty of marketing profits. To have controls on marketing channels, manufacturers in Taiwan should try to overcome obstacles by setting up marketing bases overseas and dispatching personnel to get familiar with the environment of local society in each nation in order to collect market information. They should also adopt the strategy of brand marketing and enhance product features and styles. Some have already been quite successful by adopting this strategy. Some have set show rooms and marketing bases at high points in USA. Others have set up not only marketing bases, but also distribution warehouses near Osaka, to provide speedy services. As a result, these companies not only have won praises from consumers, but also have doubled the growth in the sales volume in Japanese market. These can serve the best example for the industry. Only by

controlling marketing channels, approaching markets and collecting first-hand information, can manufacturers in Taiwan enter the international markets and stay undefeated.

A handful of other brands are worthy of mention: **Pooja** fans and sewing machines from India; **Rogaska** crystal glassware from Slovenia and **Libera** glassware from the Czech Republic; and **Royal Selangor** Pewter from Malaysia, which is already the world's biggest pewter factory.

Royal Selangor controls most of the local market for high-end gifts and has waged an aggressive overseas campaign over the past decade. Last year, 55 per cent of its turnover was in overseas markets – in 25 countries – compared with just two per cent in 1972. The company has 70 branded shops and hundreds of in-store counters worldwide. It avoids the image dilution that its hundreds of different product lines might create by emphasizing the craftsmanship passed down through generations and highlighting Malaysia's major role as a tin producer (pewter is largely made from tin). In 1999, when Interbrand did a survey of top Asian brands, Royal Selangor with its distinctive blue and gold-flecked logo was the best-known Malaysian brand, at 29th place. In 1993, Selangor bought the British silversmith, Comyns, and also set up an upmarket jeweller – with craftspeople trained by European master jewellers – in order to expand out of the pewter niche into prestige goods.

The famous **Rubik's cube** from Hungary became a truly global brand in less than two years – a remarkable achievement considering that its original launch was the result of a determined collaboration between Hungarian and American partners across the Iron Curtain. Over a hundred million cubes were probably sold – many of them, alas, unofficial copies of the authentic cube – between the product's launch in 1980 and when the global craze finally died down in around 1982.

And all of this without any marketing or promotion whatsoever: a point worth pondering for any entrepreneur considering building a global brand who doesn't happen to have tens of millions of dollars to spare for advertising.

Software, IT services and hardware

The networking of business has provided a major boost to companies in developing markets, and many new international service and product brands have emerged from South and East Asia, Eastern and Central Europe and the Baltic States in recent decades.

One important lesson from the IT boom is that there is the potential for global *service* brands to develop out of emerging markets where technical skills and educational and linguistic standards are high, yet labour is relatively cheap: call centres, web services, internet design, software design, programming, after-sales service and so forth.

In this way, some companies in emerging markets are beginning to escape from the straightjacket of manual processes, of assembly and manufacture, and take part in the 'knowledge economy' which, until recently, has been the exclusive province of the North; many of the clients of these service businesses are still the big American, European and Japanese corporations, but it's a more equal, less anonymous kind of service. The service providers have their own powerful brands – albeit business-to-business brands which are unknown to the end users of the products which their clients or their clients' clients make – and some of them are outgrowing all but the very biggest of those clients.

It's certainly one of the great benefits of the IT revolution that, unlike any previous industrial revolution, this one requires no massive investment in plant or factories, and is thus the most democratic of revolutions. Education and vision are the primary factors.

Almost everybody knows the story of **Infosys** of Bangalore in India, which rocketed to global fame in 1999 as the first Indian company ever to be listed on NASDAQ; in 2001, the company posted over US $400 million in annual revenues, and, as a profitable services company based on a sound business model, has remained relatively unscathed by the bursting of the technology bubble. Infosys now has offices around the world, and in 2001 was voted India's most admired company by the *Economic Times*.

And Infosys is a good corporate citizen, as befits any self-respecting multinational corporation in the twenty-first century. The group is a major supporter of the Bangalore Agenda Task Force, an initiative of the regional Government of Karnataka (where Deepak Kanegaonkar's sandalwood comes from), which is giving a much-needed boost to Bangalore's health, education and infrastructure facilities.

And likewise, as everybody knows, a major software and services industry has grown up in India, much of it clustered around Bangalore; the other leading international brand-name in IT services is **Wipro**, whose Chairman, Azim Hasham Premji, briefly became the second richest man in the world in 2000.

What fewer people realise is how many pockets of IT entrepreneurship are to be found in far poorer countries. A good example of this phenomenon is **Cybersoft**, a software company in Ethiopia. The brainchild of a young entrepreneur, Assefa Dagne, Cybersoft was created out of the Department of Electrical and Computer Engineering at Addis Ababa University, with which the company still collaborates closely. Cybersoft's first major project, one of the biggest ever commissioned in Ethiopia, came less than a year after the company was founded, and enabled Dagne to employ almost half of that year's computer engineering graduates. As well as providing software solutions to government and companies throughout Ethiopia, Cybersoft has won major assignments for corporate customers in the US and Sweden.

As Dagne says, 'software by its nature is neither capital intensive nor location specific. It requires intellectual capital most and can be produced anywhere in the world where this is available. In fact, this provides an opportunity to a third world country like Ethiopia to participate internationally with both a competitive and comparative advantage provided it has made the requisite preparations'.

In the hardware field, **Legend** computers of China has about a 30 per cent share of the domestic market (which, at only four per cent of homes, or around 16 million computers, has a very long way to grow). It's unlikely that this level of dominance will remain, especially now China's membership of the WTO will make the market more open to foreign competition, but the company seems in a strong enough position to make Chairman Liu Chuanzhi's prediction credible: that from 2005, Legend will be in a position to make a bid for faster international growth, aiming to become the world's No.1 PC manufacturer within ten years or so.

In Taiwan, **Acer**, under the charismatic leadership of its Chief Executive, Stan Shih, has become one of the ten biggest global PC brands since its foundation in 1976, and is certainly Taiwan's most famous brand. In their portrait of Shih,[28] Fons Trompenaars and Charles Hampden-Turner describe Acer's globalization strategy in the following terms:

'The firm started in small, but growing, markets that were not immediately interesting for the big players – markets where Acer could win with fewer resources. Thus, Acer managed to obtain top market positions in countries such as South Africa, Malaysia, the Middle East, several Latin American countries, India, and Russia. These are countries that were not seen as priorities by American, European, and Japanese major PC firms. The strategy worked out well, and Acer became a global player by starting from the periphery ... Stan Shih developed his strategy as a *response* to the moves of the bigger players, gaining undefended ground and growing *with* the often rapid rates of economic development in emerging economies. Because computerization is an important part of infrastructure development, these emerging nations would associate Acer with their own economic 'miracles' and breakthroughs, and Acer could become a permanent, even traditional, part of their growth and strength.'

Other names worth a mention are **Dimension Data** of South Africa, a leading global player in web services and networking infrastructure which has so far managed to weather the technology storm; **DATI** of Latvia, one of the largest software developers in Eastern Europe, specializes in large-scale software project design and development, and is the largest company in a promising cluster of over 500 companies in and around Riga. As with the Bangalore cluster and several similar ones throughout the developing world where there are sufficient levels of education, infrastructure, funding, and government support, the client is still usually an American or Western European-owned multinational corporation; but this is service-provision of a kind that many thousands of companies in developed countries strive to deliver.

Other service brands

Other kinds of service businesses can create their own valuable international brands – in law, consulting and other professional services, education, advertising, design, tourism and hospitality and so forth.

Even though the audiences for some of these brands are unavoidably limited, they can still be highly influential. One good example of this is the **Bled School of Management** in Slovenia, a graduate school which has earned a reputation which ranks it alongside the London Business School, INSEAD and other similar institutions. Since its foundation, the school has offered more than 700 programmes to around 24 000 managers; participants have come from more than 50 countries and 3 200 companies and multinational organizations. It's the only institute of global standing to be based in an emerging market, and to a sizeable and influential international elite, it does a great deal to enhance the reputation of Slovenia as a whole, as well as training the next generation of managers for the country's own corporations.

It is in the service industries, and in particular in educational and creative services, where the unique cultural profile of a country can count more than its size or wealth. Several web design agencies in South-Eastern Europe, for example, are currently doing good business in the Far East (one Slovene company has recently opened a subsidiary in Tokyo), and this is apparently because there is a type of edgy, no-holds-barred creativity which comes quite naturally to young Balkan designers one generation too young to have experienced Socialist rule, and is entirely alien in a more collectivist, more ordered society like Japan. In businesses where originality counts for a great deal – like design – this degree of radical unfamiliarity is of enormous and marketable value. The notion of a country leveraging its cultural differences to give its service brands competitive advantage, even in upstream export markets, is most interesting.

The phenomenon can also be seen in the hospitality industries, where the brand promise of the company is very often based on some cultural characteristic, real or perceived, of the people in the company's home country – hotel chains, resorts, airlines, and so forth. International hotel brands from emerging markets include **Oberoi** hotels of India, **Taj Group** hotels of India (another division of the Tata group), **Banyan Tree** and **Shangri-La** hotels, which play very successfully on the perception of gentle, exotic, considerate hospitality which their home countries enjoy amongst Western consumers. It's exactly the same associative mechanism which, over the years, was used to turn **Singapore Airlines** into a major global brand.

Most major tourist resorts in emerging countries function, or need to function, as international brands: even though they remain physically based in the domestic market, they must be marketed in, and be available from, pretty much everywhere else on earth if they are to remain competitive. Since, unlike the majority of other brands I have described in this chapter, they directly represent the physical reality of their home country, they play a very important part in communicating national identity and national values around the world, even to the majority of people who will never use them. Examples of such resorts are the **Deer Park** in Sri Lanka, **Serena** hotels in Kenya and Tanzania (although, with hotels in Pakistan as well, this group qualifies as a distributed international brand as well), **Treetops** in Kenya, and many others.

And almost every emerging market has at least one international brand in the shape of its national airline, and it is equally common for these brands to base their service promise on some cultural trait of the country in question, as did Singapore Airlines. National airlines are often, very aptly, referred to as the 'flag-carriers' of their home country, and although they are only rarely profitable and privately-owned or privately managed enterprises, they play an indisputably important role in branding their country. Whether they like it or not, they broadcast a very strong impression of the hospitality, competence, technical ability, time-keeping, cuisine, linguistic and cultural flexibility, wealth, education, taste and style of their home country and its inhabitants, and as such are one of the most powerful communicators of national identity available to any country.

Branded industrial goods

Not all brands, of course, are for consumers, and there are many powerful industrial and business-to-business brands which the shopper on the street has never heard of in his or her life; yet their power, within their sphere of influence, is in almost every way identical to the power of consumer brands over end users.

The professional purchasers and specifiers in large organizations, whose job it is to buy supplies and materials for their companies, take pride in denying that they are swayed by anything as ethereal as brand values or as superficial as marketing: yet their purchasing patterns show that in their jobs they accept brand equity in lieu of first-hand experience in exactly the same way as they do when they're buying shampoo in a supermarket on their way home from the office.

Success stories from such brands in developing markets include names like **Cemex** cement of Mexico: one of the world's biggest names in cement and certainly the most profitable, Cemex's operating cash flow has grown by a yearly average of 20 per cent during the past 10 years; and for each of the last 10 years, their margin has exceeded 30 per cent. Cemex now has operations in Mexico, the USA, Venezuela and Dominican Republic, Colombia, Central America and the Caribbean, Spain, Egypt, the Philippines and Indonesia.

Probably the only aircraft manufacturer from an emerging market with a well-known international name is **Embraer** of Brazil, the world's second-largest producer of smaller commercial jet aircraft. Embraer is one of the exceptions which prove the rule about Brazilian companies rarely exporting products under their own names: this is one of the rare cases where Brazilian-designed, Brazilian-funded and Brazilian-made products are exported around the world in finished form. Aircraft manufacture makes even more money for Brazil than iron-ore exports, for many decades Brazil's principal foreign currency earner, and all this is due to Embraer, which makes Brazil the fourth largest exporter of aircraft in the world. I should add that the way in which the company is subsidized by its government – and by which it was originally owned – is deemed to be in contravention of WTO rules and causes frequent disagreements with Embraer's overseas competitors.

DPL Gloves of Sri Lanka is, in many ways, a typical example of a highly successful manufacturer which *doesn't* brand its own products, and for very understandable reasons. Founded in 1976, DPL is the fifth largest glove manufacturer in the world. Specializing in natural and synthetic latex based domestic and industrial gloves, DPL services nearly five per cent of the global market. It operates four manufacturing locations in Sri Lanka, and produces over half a million gloves per day. DPL is also ISO 9002 accredited. If you buy a pair of washing-up gloves somewhere in the world, there's a good chance they will be manufactured by DPL but carry somebody else's brand name.

DPL faces the classic supplier's dilemma: its margins and growth could be much increased and its business less vulnerable to competitors if it could make the investment in developing its own brand names, but in doing so it would risk losing its entire client base, who might very understandably desert DPL the instant they suspected that their humble supplier was trying to go into competition with them.

There is no question that the whole culture and mentality of a supplier company is entirely different from that of a brand-owner, and some kind of revolution has to occur before such a change can happen and a company decide that it's worth taking the risk of such a move.

Kamthorn and Panudda Kamthornthip of Cha-Lom in Bangkok faced exactly the same dilemma: by producing their own brand, they knew there was a risk that their US clients would drop them. In the event, this didn't happen, and it shows that a good supplier is a valued resource, and a customer's loyalty may override such considerations. Perhaps it also shows that Cha-Lom's clients in far-off America neither knew nor cared whether their manufacturers in Thailand were developing their own brand; or perhaps they did know but simply didn't consider a brand like BeBe-Bushh to be a rival in any sense of the word. And of course, in the short term, they would have been right: it is no kind of rival to an Osh Kosh or a Gap Kids, and the very idea is laughable. But who knows what kind of a threat they might pose in the longer term?

For now, DPL's culture is overtly and unmistakably that of the supplier, albeit a very ambitious one: their publicity states that:

DPL's Corporate Plan envisages a five fold expansion of its glove manufacturing activities by year 2005. Stemming from our culture to be close to our customers, the cornerstone of this plan has been identified as the attainment of Preferred Supplier status with our customers.

As long as their business is stable and profitable, it would be quite pointless to launch into a risky and uncertain venture as a brand-owner, a field in which they have no experience, and without the distribution, retail relationships and marketing dollars of their rivals.

It may be another factor in the equation that the Sri Lankan culture, like many highly collectivist societies, is somewhat biased against producing Western-style entrepreneurs: the way that Sri Lankan children are educated at home and at school tends to emphasize the virtues of faithful and scrupulous service to others, rather than aggression, ambition or self-aggrandizement. Nonetheless, the hundreds of successful Japanese and Korean brands show that there is an equally potent model of brand-building, borne out of a sense of collective ambition and loyalty, which suits such cultures every bit as well as the CEO-led culture suits highly individualistic societies.

But supposing a way could be found to combine the two – to develop the branded business alongside the unbranded, without the one threatening the other – and with the full knowledge, approval and even support of their Western clients? And supposing such an arrangement were one that the Western client company actively sought, because it added to their own reputation and enhanced their ethical credentials? This is a notion to which I will return in Chapter 4.

Several of the industrial brands whose names consumers do know have gained their fame in less illustrious ways – Semtex plastic explosive is a Czech invention, the Russian Kalashnikov is one of the best-known manufacturer's names in the world. Such anomalies occur because wars and terrorist acts receive more exhaustive and detailed coverage by the world's media than any other phenomenon, so any brand names caught in there will inevitably receive the kind of intense and prolonged exposure which money simply couldn't buy. For the same reason, almost everybody still knows the name of Molotov, long after his deeds have been forgotten.

And one major B2B brand from Taiwan, the home of Acer, is **Evergreen Marine**, one of the largest container shipping groups in the world, with some 130 ships to its name. Dr Chang Yung-fa, who founded the company in 1968, has built the Evergreen Group into a major international organization whose affiliate companies are active in shipping and port operations, aviation, road transport, hotels and engineering. More than just another example of how an emerging economy can benefit from the business dynamics of globalization, Evergreen is indisputably part of the backbone of global trade itself.

Cosmetics and pharmaceuticals

In 1971 Dr. Victor Hettigoda borrowed 2 500 Rupees (around 55 euros) from a relative and went into business. He devised, manufactured, bottled, labelled and packaged his own formula of Ayurvedic Balm and carried it around to the local village shops in Sri Lanka, where he persuaded the shopkeepers to stock it and promote it to their customers.

His efforts bore results and in time **Siddhalepa** became a household name throughout the sub-continent. He gradually expanded his business into a multi-million dollar company and today his group of companies – the Hettigoda Group – has a workforce of over 1500 people, and produces over 70 Ayurvedic Herbal preparations which are exported to the USA, UK, Germany, Switzerland, Japan, Italy, Hong Kong, Singapore, UAE and elsewhere. Hettigoda Industries was the first Ayurvedic Drug Manufacturing Company in Asia to be awarded ISO 9002 and ISO 9001.

Some of Siddhalepa's many sub-brands are worth listing if for no other reason than their wonderful-sounding names: **Supirivicky** Herbal Toothpaste, **Visaka** Herbal Soap, **Threepala** Digestive Supplement, **Garlic-in-Bee-Honey** Dietary Supplement, **Maduthala** Herbal Mosquito Repellent, **Lakpeyawa** Herbal Tea and eight other varieties of herbal teas, **Dasamularishta**, **Ashwagandarishta**, **Draksharishta** and 10 other varieties of arishta, **Mahanarayanaya**, **Mahasiddharta**, **Vishnu Eranda** and **Neelyadi** Herbal Massage Oils, **Peenas Thailaya**, and **Asamodagam Arka** Herbal Gripe Water.

In one sense, it's not surprising that this category is a rich one: if part of the appeal of emerging-market brands in the West is that they are connected to a richer, older, wiser culture than our own, then medicines and folk products of all kinds are bound to have a special appeal. Their humble country of origin, rather than being a surprising fact which consumers decide to overlook, is actually what they are looking for in the first place.

One company which deserves a special mention is **O Boticário** (Brazil), which is, together with Embraer and Marcopolo, another of the very few exceptions to the tendency of Brazilian companies not to export their brands. The company was founded in the 1970s, and is today the largest (and one of the very few) independent cosmetics companies operating in the Brazilian market. With over 350 different cosmetics and perfumes, O Boticário's products are distributed through more than 1 000 franchisees all over Brazil. O Boticário products have been available in Portugal since 1985; they are sold in smaller numbers in Bolivia, Peru and Paraguay (with ambitious plans to expand further throughout South America); and they are also available at around 400 points of sale in Japan. The company has funded its own not-for-profit conservation foundation since 1990, the Fundação O Boticário de Proteção à Natureza, which is today recognized as one of Brazil's most active and influential organizations in ecology and sustainability.

One can't help feeling, looking at O Boticário's range, that if the company could create an export range with a little more focus on national identity, it might have a stronger international brand. The names and imagery of its products are Italian, French, American, Latin, Russian (**Uomini, Innamorata, One of Us, Ma Chérie, Lights, Clipping, Be a Flower, Carpe Diem, Crazy Feelings, Dimitri**), borrowing from almost every culture under the sun apart from Brazilian (which is presumably not considered exotic enough for Brazilian consumers). The brands have an almost exclusively domestic focus, providing ersatz international glamour for Brazilian consumers, rather than Brazilian glamour for international consumers. This seems like a missed opportunity, as the company's Brazilian heritage, combined with the genuine ethical story which can be told around the Fundação O Boticário, could combine to create a very attractive and powerful brand story (ecology, wild nature, magic herbal properties, rainforest imagery, youth, beauty, sex appeal, carnival spirit – the *authentic* Brazilian Body Shop, in other words) which is resonant, meaningful and appealing to consumers in Europe, North America and Asia.

Other brands which have enjoyed international success in this field include **Shahnaz Herbal** (India), **Tiger Balm** (Singapore), **White Flower Oil** (China) and many others besides.

But emerging countries don't only produce charming folk remedies. The antibiotic **Sumamed** (azithromycin) was invented, developed, produced and marketed by the Pliva company of Croatia and is the world's top selling antibiotic in its class. Pliva has over 400 other patents in its possession and wholly-owned subsidiaries in 25 countries.

Tata

The Tata corporation of India comprises, among other assets, Asia's largest software exporter (**Tata Consultancy Services**), the world's sixth largest manufacturer brand of watches (**Titan**), India's largest private sector steel producer (**Tata Steel**), the largest 5-star chain of luxury hotels in India (**Taj Group Hotels**), not to mention India's largest manufacturer of soda ash and India's largest private sector power utility.

The corporation also owns the world's largest integrated tea operation, **Tata Tetley**, following their recent acquisition of the Tetley Tea Company of England, the world's second-largest teabag manufacturer – a spectacular reversal of the traditional arrangement, where the tea is grown in a poor country, and sold at a low price to a brand-owner in a rich country, who sells it on to rich consumers at a vastly higher price.

Tata's original export strategy for Titan watches was to start down-hill, and concentrate on markets where there was already a large non-resident Indian or India-friendly population. The Middle East was chosen partly because the Arabian Gulf benefits from a certain amount of 'media overspill' from Indian television stations, so little additional marketing budget was required. Rapid growth of sales here helped build volumes and revenues for expansion into newer territories.

When it came to Europe, the company needed to change its style of marketing and delivery quite substantially. This involved a complete reworking of its business model to speed up delivery times, and also bringing in European designers and ad agencies, plus a major marketing spend to position Titan as *The New World Watch*, stressing the French collaboration, Swiss engineering, European designers and Japanese know-how which went into its products.

At present, export sales only account for eight per cent of the company's turnover, but like Tata's other major consumer brands, Taj Group Hotels and Tata Tetley, foreign markets have been identified as a primary source of the company's future growth.

As R.K. Krishna Kumar, the Chairman of Tata Tetley, Vice Chairman of Tata Tea, and Managing Director of the Taj Group of Hotels says:

> 'We wanted to create a global brand, because the marketplace was global and in a global marketplace only global brands survive; local players get marginalized. We did not want to get marginalized, so we had to either build a global brand or acquire one. Building a global brand was very expensive, so we acquired one.'

Very few companies in emerging markets are in a position to talk so lightly of acquiring a multi-million dollar enterprise to boost their brand credentials, but the rationale is precisely the same whether we're talking about Tata in India or Cybersoft in Ethiopia: poor countries don't have to be the victims of globalization. By understanding and harnessing the power of brands – which are the only way for companies to retain enough profile to be competitive in a world-sized marketplace – poorer states can use the rules of globalization in their favour, just as the First World has always done.

CHAPTER 4

The challenge of branded exports

Looking at the list of companies in the previous chapter, several principles begin to emerge which could be of value to other companies attempting to export from developing countries, and to governments which want to create a favourable environment for such companies to flourish.

Some of the lessons which emerge most frequently and powerfully are these:

1. A good way to gain a foothold in overseas markets and start to build critical mass is by selling to diaspora populations, as Jollibee have done with expatriate Filipinos in Hong Kong, the Middle East and United States, and Titan and Satnam with non-resident Indians in the Gulf States, USA, UK and elsewhere. The lowered or non-existent linguistic and cultural barriers, as well as a certain amount of media overspill, mean that the task is somewhat lightened.

2. Even where there is no suitable expatriate population, it makes sense to start in markets where there is some common cultural or linguistic heritage (as Brazilian brands like Pau de Azucar and O Boticário have found in Portugal).

   It is always easier to target 'downhill' markets first, before launching an attack on first world markets. All consumers, without even realising it, see other countries according to an unspoken but nonetheless very real hierarchy: some countries are perceived as having lower status (usually because they're poorer or less stable or less attractive in some way); some are equal; and some are perceived as aspirational country-brands, usually because they're richer or happier or more attractive. Imported brands are therefore ranked in the consumer's mind, to some extent, according to where the consumer believes they come from. So a brand from an aspirational country will be judged aspirational, and consumers will expect it to be expensive and desirable, and feel that owning it will add to their social standing. For example, most consumers in the Czech Republic will view American brands are 'above them', and are therefore predisposed to perceive them as aspirational and desirable, and will expect them to be expensive. The same consumers will view Bulgarian brands as 'below them' and will expect them to be cheaper, so they will probably not consider buying them unless it's a price-driven purchase and they want to save money.

Companies like Laško and Techo, which understand clearly where they stand in this worldwide perceptual pecking-order, and make sensible use of it, can save themselves a great deal of effort and money by harnessing positive existing consumer perceptions of their country of origin. And as the Acer case shows, an additional benefit of concentrating on other emerging markets first is that they are themselves growing markets, and exporters can benefit from this rising tide.

3. A bolder alternative strategy is for a company to attempt to establish itself directly in the market which is perceived to be the world capital of its product category. It's immeasurably harder at the start, and certain to be far more expensive, even if there's an abundance of higher-income consumers to be found, but it's all downhill from there: and the brand will pick up enormously valuable equities by association on the way. Launching Urvâshi in Paris was a classic case of 'starting at the top'.

4. If a new brand's country of origin is decidedly negative or inappropriate, it's better to be realistic, and wait until the brand itself has accumulated sufficient reputation and market share for it to be safe to begin communicating where it comes from. This was Nokia's strategy, and Titan watches have pursued a similar route.

5. Products with a 'lateral link' to the popular image of their country of origin can often gain extra standout and brand equity as a result: most people would hardly notice a new Russian vodka, but the appeal of a Russian gaming computer probably fed off decades of imagery created by spy films, and ensured instant cult status for Cybiko. Less controversial, but equally noticeable, are ice-hockey sticks from Estonia (it's a cold, Northern country after all), pewter from Malaysia (not the first place that springs to mind for luxury goods, but it is where the best tin comes from), and beer from Slovenia (it may be part of ex-Yugoslavia now, but the brand dates back from the days of the Austro-Hungarian Empire).

6. Acquiring a defunct brand from a first-world country can sometimes prove a cost-effective way of acquiring brand equity in a hurry.

This presumably wasn't Royal Enfield's game-plan in 1949, but the company's success might be profitably replicated by others: an emerging-market company buys an unwanted brand from a rich country and allows it to recover and convalesce back home, where the environment is more favourable, competition is less fierce, the conditions which caused its downfall in Europe or America don't exist, and consumers may well look up to the brand rather than down on it. Even if the awareness of the brand may be low to zero in the emerging market, the assets are well worth having: ready-made second hand TV commercials, corporate identity programmes and designs, learning and experience (embodied in key people, who might even be prepared to relocate with the brand in return for greater responsibility and a stake in the business, and who would otherwise lose their jobs), perhaps even production facilities, machine tools, quality control systems and so forth. The brand can be nursed back to life as a new domestic brand in the emerging market, gain strength, vitality, a new character, and in due course return to the original market and the world stage.

Very often, absence makes the heart grow fonder, so consumers in the brand's original home market will be glad to see it back and may have forgotten why it failed: residual brand loyalty and per-haps even nostalgia will kick in (as was the case with Royal Enfield); overheads will have been greatly lowered and the company made tougher; the original owners (if they have any sense) will have retained a share and can help to re-establish the company in the original country, and it will return to fight another day.

One could even envisage such a 'brand recovery' service becom-ing a speciality of the right kind of company in the right kind of emerging market.

7. Where infrastructure for launching an international business is really basic or non-existent, then mould the business around what-ever other parts of the social fabric are more stable and fertile, like providing a climbing plant with a cane – for example, Cybersoft building the company in close partnership with Addis Ababa University. Even a government department might prove a suitable 'cane' in some circumstances.

8. Use media overspill: as a preliminary exercise to selecting overseas target markets and communications strategies, it is well worth con-sidering where the channels of communication are easiest to access and cheapest to use. In cases of TV overspill, they may come as a free bonus with domestic media spend.

9. Pick a product area where brand equity, rather than manufacturing quality or price, is a major component of product appeal, such as luxury goods or fashion. It is always easier for multinational corpo-rations, with their massive financial resources, to outdo challengers in the realms of product quality and innovation, or to undercut their

prices. Where it is sometimes harder for them to win every time (and where they may be less interested in competing, because of the smaller opportunity) is in the outer edges of perceptual advantage – niche appeals, unusual countries of origin, anything that runs contrary to the mainstream of mass-market brands.

10. Younger consumers, with their insatiable appetite for things which are as different as possible from the mainstream products their parents prefer, are a rich potential target for unusual products from unusual places. Students, for example, are the most likely target for a product like Roustam Tariko's Russian banking brand, for the simple reason that it provides the starkest possible contrast to the 'sensible' brands targeted at their parents' generation. The selection of a brand can often be a form of protest or non-conformism, even if this sometimes looks perilously close to 'cutting off your nose to spite your face'.

The challenges and difficulties

There are plenty of examples of companies in poor and emerging markets which are starting to achieve their ambitions of marketing their brands in the West; and there are plenty of valuable lessons which they can teach us.

Whether this trend is set to continue, or whether it will remain the exception rather than the rule, is hard to say: but it seems likely that once the domestic competitors of companies like Gandh Sugandh, Russki Standard, Cha-Lom, Shanghai Tang, Elan and Haier have seen the growth which a branded export business creates, many of them will be tempted to follow the same path.

However, it would be doing the remarkable entrepreneurs behind these companies a disservice to understate the challenges they face in building a branded business overseas.

The basic obstacles are familiar to anybody who has ever tried to export a product: identifying the markets with the greatest potential; managing the complexities of foreign exchange; getting distribution and retail presence abroad and striking the right deal with the right local partners; producing and shipping the right quantity of the right product at the right quality to the right market at the right moment; marketing it effectively despite major differences in consumer culture, managing tricky issues like after-sales service, obtaining the necessary permissions and licences to export from the home market and import into the target market and so forth.

Any exporter of *branded* goods will face a range of additional challenges which are mainly to do with maintaining control over brand image at a distance. Because a brand's value depends so much on showing a coherent and consistent personality to the consumer, control of all the marketing messages becomes essential: yet it's extremely hard to achieve from afar. The price at which the product is sold, the way in which it is presented to the consumer at the point of sale, the way it's marketed and advertised – all of these are hard enough to achieve at home, let alone in a distant country.

It's equally difficult protecting the all-important intellectual property rights of a brand, especially since agreements like TRIPS (Trade-Related Aspects of Intellectual-Property rights), the WTO's attempt to establish a worldwide standard for the legal protection of intellectual property, are widely and rightly criticized as being biased against poorer countries, many of which find them too expensive to comply with. Nonetheless, it is essential for exporters to prevent other companies from producing 'me-too' brands, with misleadingly similar names, designs or packaging – for as soon as a new product begins to achieve any success in the marketplace, there are many rival companies waiting to see whether consumers like it, and ready to offer them something similar at a lower price, or with an enhanced specification, or more easily available.

These difficulties and traps may seem daunting enough between countries with similar levels of sophistication, but they are *massively* intensified when the direction of export is from poor country to rich.

Selling products from one mature market economy into another – say, from America to Germany – is like pushing a heavy load over level ground: you need some initial momentum, but once you get things moving, the difficulties gradually diminish. The basic compatibility of the legal, financial and logistical systems in both countries, often harmonized and perfected over decades or even centuries of bilateral trade, makes exporting fairly plain sailing. What's more, there may be relatively few cultural disconnects between the sophisticated Western consumers at home and the sophisticated Western consumers abroad, which makes the marketing of the brand altogether more straightforward – sometimes, it may even be as simple as taking the domestic advertising campaign and translating it into the relevant language.[29]

Selling goods from a developed market economy into a poorer country – say, from Canada to Mexico – has traditionally felt more like pushing a load downhill. There may be incompatibilities in the way things are organized in each country; care needs to be exercised to ensure that the brand's copyright is properly protected in countries where such subtleties as intellectual property rights are not widely respected; and the basic economics of selling at a price which the market can afford need to be worked out; but the product itself is almost bound to appeal in a country where such sophisticated products are less common, and a rich country of origin often adds glamour and appeal to the product, giving it a head start over domestic competitors. International trade agreements have typically favoured and facilitated trade of this and the previous type, and their 'bilateralism' has been heavily geared to the assumption that branded goods travel from rich to rich and rich to poor, but only raw materials and labour travel from poor to rich.

But selling goods from a poorer country into a highly-developed Western market economy – from Sri Lanka to America, or Kenya to Italy – really does feel like pushing a load up a steep hill, with every imaginable force of law, prejudice, wealth, consumer perception, geography, tariffs, currency and logistics working against you.

An export manual used by companies in California looking to sell their products abroad has this to say on the subject:

> If your product has sold reasonably well in the US, chances are it will also sell abroad. Why? Because, to do well here, the world's largest market, you've already proven you can compete, not only against other American products, but imported products as well.

The truth of this statement can hardly be denied. Products which have been developed and sold in rich countries are battle-hardened, and as long as they're properly priced and effectively distributed and marketed, they can literally wipe out the domestic competition in any poor country where they end up.

The story of global marketing is one of highly sophisticated brands, honed to perfection in tough domestic markets like America or Germany, which, when they first appear in less advanced countries, encounter very little serious competition. For many years, these brands also met with relatively little resistance from consumers – the products had instant appeal in countries where consumers were still unused to powerful marketing techniques, glossy advertising images, and weren't yet 'inoculated' against the marketer's armoury. However, this effect has become steadily less apparent as consumers in poorer countries have become more adept at identifying and screening out commercial messages, just as we learned to do decades ago in the West.

Over the years, as more and more Western brands have launched in emerging markets, the contest has become less one of imported brands against domestic brands, and more and more a battle between rival Western brands for the hearts, minds and purses of consumers. National brands tend to be bought up by the Western brand-owners in an attempt to attach reassuring, culturally appropriate brand values to the imported product, or are relegated to downmarket, cut-price substitutes for the consumers who can't afford the higher prices of imported brands.

A side-effect of this process is that it raises consumers' standards and expectations, along with the general standard of all products in the marketplace. In fact, as I mentioned in Chapter 2, the domestic manufacturers which are not bought out by the German or American or Japanese brand-owners may, in time, become strengthened by this process – if it doesn't drive them out of business.

The phenomenon which this book identifies is partly the result of this process: now, through long exposure to the competition generated by imported Western brands, manufacturers in some developing markets are themselves so highly developed that they can entertain the notion of exporting back to rich countries. Possibly this 'return match' is one effect which the multinational corporations didn't anticipate when they first began exporting to the third world all those years ago.

Raising finance

In my conversations with the emerging entrepreneurs described in the previous chapter, the difficulty of getting funding for their export venture occurs over and over again. Deepak Kanegaonkar, for example, tells of the reaction of one Indian banker he approached with his plan to produce India's first export perfume and sell it in Paris:

> He said: 'look, when you spray the perfume it vanishes into thin air. I can't see it, I can't catch it – so how can I finance it?' I don't understand that – he seemed to think that you can only finance bricks and walls.

Kanegaonkar had to invest $3 million of his company's own funds in developing Urvâshi: a huge sum even for a successful business in India, yet this is small change compared to the budgets of the major French perfume labels against which Urvâshi has to compete. But the brand's initial success in France caused the Indian government to take notice, and in 2000, a consortium of banks led by the Export–Import Bank of India granted Deepak a long-term $5 million loan to build his brand abroad.

It's not surprising if the sophistication of the venture capital market is about the same as – or lower than – the state of the market for branded products in any given country, and investment funds tend to become widely available in an industry only when there are clear precedents for successful investment. Nobody much likes to back a pioneer.[30]

However, there are other ways around the problem, and no shortage of development funds, grants and philanthropic investment sources for suitable projects in emerging countries. One of the most important of these is the International Finance Corporation, a division of the World Bank: the IFC is the largest multilateral source of loan and equity financing for private sector projects in the developing world.

The most natural source of external capital for would-be brand exporters in developing markets is foreign direct investment by overseas corporations, and most emerging countries have some kind of strategy in place for courting and developing FDI. However, the kind of FDI which they envisage is typically the establishment of offshore manufacturing bases by foreign brand-owners, or the acquisition of supplier companies to support their own businesses – not making pure venture investments directly into local companies with aspirations to build their *own* global brands.

A Western brand-owner might also think twice about backing an exporter which, if successful, could become a competitor to their own branded products back home – unless, as I will show later in this chapter, they could position the funding as an 'ethical' investment.

Even where such investments are available to aspiring domestic exporters, like all equity investments, it's a trade-off: the company gets funding and possibly also expertise, but its ownership and control are both diminished. Whether this trade-off is worth making depends very much on the sensitivity and vision of the investors: if they force products developed in emerging markets to be copy-cat, cut-price versions of Western brands, then they may do them more harm than good in the long term.

In order to encourage FDI, the governments of most developing nations will offer foreign corporations all manner of tax incentives and grants, build industrial estates and export processing zones for them; they will attempt to simplify the bureaucratic procedures facing potential investors; they negotiate bilateral tax, trade, and investment treaties with countries from wherever investments might come; they attempt to create a favourable environment by guaranteeing repatriation of profits, assuring access to imported components and promising not to expropriate property without compensation. No doubt they are partly influenced by the desire to 'acquire' a prestigious Northern brand and link it publicly with their own national brand.

Now, all of this support may be designed for the convenience of foreign companies, but it undoubtedly also creates an environment where domestic companies with international ambitions can flourish – assuming, of course, that they are allowed access to the support. In an ideal world, such companies would be offered *enhanced* access to such facilities and even greater privileges and tax breaks than the foreign companies, but it is rarely so.

The role of government in encouraging and facilitating the development of export brands is clearly critical, and is a subject I will talk about more in Chapter 5. Suffice to say at this point that if a country is going to start reducing its dependence on the sale of unbranded, low-margin commodities for generating foreign income, and make a move towards high-margin branded goods and services, this must clearly be a nationwide project, promoted, guided, supported and driven by central government.

Making do with less

Although the question of funding is obviously crucial to the success of these ventures, it is worth mentioning that the total cost of developing a branded business overseas need not be as great as conventional wisdom dictates – at least not in the early stages.

For a start, it is seldom necessary or advisable for a first-time exporter to launch in more than one overseas market at a time (few first-time exporters have the resources to do this anyway), and a limited test-marketing exercise is almost always the most sensible way to start. Limited funding for such an initiative is easier to obtain, and further funding, if the test proves successful, correspondingly straightforward.

And there is plenty of good advice to be had on developing a brand at relatively low cost – multi-million dollar advertising campaigns are unlikely to be the first approach of an emerging exporter.

One way to promote a product without spending a fortune on it is by effective PR rather than through advertising in paid-for media – if the brand and its owner have their own compelling and genuinely unusual story (emerging global brands from unexpected and exotic countries will have this, almost by definition), it should be possible to generate valuable publicity simply through editorial coverage and the resulting word of mouth.

Journalists in rich countries could well be more interested in stories like this than yet another rich-country, rich-company brand; and it is important for brand-owners in emerging markets to be quite clear about which aspects of their own story appear most exotic to people in other countries – no matter how banal they may seem back home. The fact that Russki Standard boasted the only vodka recipe personally approved by Tsar Nicholas; or that the real sandalwood essence in Urvâshi had never before been permitted to leave the country by the Indian government; or that Kamthorn Kamthornthip had spent the last fifteen years manufacturing for Gap Kids before creating his own brand in the same factory – these are the kinds of stories which journalists know their readers will find interesting, and publicity is always free when this is so. They are also the kinds of detail-rich communications which suit informative editorial, but are very hard to get across in paid-for advertising media.

Whatever the medium, the basic rule of consistency in brand-building will always apply. Consumers, especially in rich countries, are bombarded with so many advertising messages in a day, and have so little spare time and attention to give new arrivals in the stores, that a new product's only hope of registering on their consciousness is the consistent reiteration of a simple, unchanging, yet compelling and unusual message.

Small armies can defeat large armies, if only their soldiers march precisely in step. Big budgets can be totally wasted through inconsistent marketing communications, yet small budgets can be surprisingly effective through absolute commitment to a sufficiently bold and striking message.

And the message, especially if it's not backed by a huge budget, tends to be far more effective if it arrives by an unexpected route or appears in an unusual context – so time spent on creative media planning with a local expert, as early as possible in the process, is almost always a sound investment. It's all too easy to spend large sums on creating highly noticeable marketing communications materials, and then seriously diminish their effectiveness by burying them in the same media where the competition also advertise. The obvious media is often the most expensive media, so any truly lateral thinking on this front is usually well worth the effort.

Media 'accidents' – where the footprint of domestic advertising media happens to overspill into another country – can sometimes help export brands, as we have seen, and it's worth giving some time to thinking about how to leverage this. It is one of the reasons, for example, why marketing to a diaspora population is relatively straightforward, since so many of them will be tuned into the domestic TV channels of their home countries via satellite.

A case in point is satellite TV spillover from India (primarily via the Star TV network), which has enabled many Indian products, ranging from foodstuffs to clothing to cosmetics and even cars, to gain export markets in the Middle East, Africa and some South East Asian markets, most of which are much richer economies (and have much higher per capita incomes). Unlike the Indian market, many of these countries have no restrictions on imports of foreign goods, and several Indian brands have thus discovered, almost by accident, that they can compete quite successfully with international brands.

Most of the owners of these brands were initially unprepared for the effects of this overspill and weren't equipped to respond appropriately (the export habits of Indian companies tend to be driven by production criteria, and pricing for export is typically lower than domestic, both because of marginal costing and also due to some incentives and tax rebates which the Indian government offers to exporters). Their advertising was and continues to be aimed primarily at the Indian consumer, but more recently has begun to show some awareness of its expanded audience.

There are other cases in which the international branding of products is truly accidental – as a result of terrestrial TV or radio channels which are picked up in neighbouring countries, tourists being exposed to domestic campaigns while visiting countries and so forth. The more and more commonplace phenomenon of product placement in Hollywood movies creates its own overspill: in some cases, the featured product isn't readily available outside the USA, but the movie is distributed worldwide.

There are other ways in which a brand can emerge onto the international market without any deliberate promotion by the owner: for example, visitors to a country can 'discover' a domestic brand while on holiday there, and bring their demand for the product back home. Brand-owners should always be on the lookout for such opportunities: it may be just a handful of consumers with a passing interest in the brand, but it could be a way to get the ball rolling.

Last but not least, the internet offers good opportunities for boosting the fame of new brands. Even though the cost of conventional online media – banners on heavily-visited sites, for example – is hardly more cost-effective than print or broadcast media, and the bargain value of the internet's early days has pretty much disappeared, this is still the only truly global medium, and with skill and luck, can create remarkable word-of-mouth phenomena on a tiny budget. Considered as a social facilitator rather than a commercial media channel, the internet is likely to continue to offer the only real bargains in global promotion.

Studies in crazes, 'social viruses' and other such word-of-mouth phenomena[31] confirm that certain people, products, behaviours and events, from time to time, will catch the public's imagination and spread like wildfire, often without any conventional marketing support, and the internet is one channel which has helped such phenomena to become truly global. Although the processes involved are hard to isolate and generally not well understood, their mere existence confirms the belief that outsmarting the competition really is a viable alternative to outspending them when it comes to building an international brand.

Eleven levers for outsmarting the competition

Any would-be global brand produced in an emerging market is, by definition, a challenger, and challengers are seldom in a position to outspend their rivals in the marketplace. Their strength, and their rise to success, is almost always achieved through outsmarting the competition: and the techniques of outsmarting are relatively easy to list (even if they aren't always so easy to execute).

Outsmarting is exactly analogous to the function of a lever in physics: it enables a relatively small force to exert an effect which is out of proportion to its size. In my experience, there are eleven major levers which emerging-market brands can harness in order to achieve this effect:

1. **Leverage your enemy's popular support.** This powerful effect is achieved by questioning a fundamental aspect of a brand leader's appeal (such as its country of origin), and offering the consumer

a radically new alternative. Easier said than done, of course, but if the buying public do find the alternative to be more appealing, it has the effect of denting not only the brand leader's image, but also that of the dozens of 'me-too' brands which always cluster around a market leader. It is extremely hard, if not impossible, for the brand leader to remain popular for very long if one of its key equities is made to look old-fashioned or ridiculous – and of course it can't change quickly without looking foolish and undignified, having spent decades pushing that aspect of its brand.

A classic example of this type of leverage was adopted by Diesel jeans when it took on the market leader, Levi's, with something less than 10 per cent of Levi's marketing budget. By questioning the basic notion that jeans *had* to be an authentic, classic product, made in America and rooted in American culture, Diesel pulled the rug out from under the feet not only of Levi's but also Lee, Wrangler, and dozens of other competitors whose brand promises were basically 'we're as authentic and American as Levi's'. Diesel jeans appeared to come from nowhere, and their only references to American heritage were heavily ironic.[32]

As is so often the case with this type of lever, the vulnerable part of Levi's audience was the younger generation of consumers who were being expected to buy into a brand promise which they simply inherited from their parents' generation. The company hadn't succeeded in earning the respect of these younger consumers, who in any case didn't much want to wear the same brands as their parents, and were already on the lookout for an alternative. Both inside and outside America, this generation was also one of the first to start questioning the absolute appeal of 'brand America', so a label which cocked a snook at the whole idea of the 'Authentic American' jeans brand was absolutely in tune with their changing loyalties.

An emerging-market brand which questions the unquestioned – such as whether perfumes have to come from France or Italy, whether running shoes have to be American or European, whether hi-fi has to be Japanese – is taking a big gamble. But if it has correctly read the buying public's latent desire for something fresh, it may find itself propelled into a market position which is out of all proportion to its marketing spend, for the simple reason that the huge weight of the market leader's popular appeal is now working against its own interests, and for the newcomer's.

2. **Leverage the effect of detail.** I will describe this point and several of the others which follow in more detail in the next chapter, because they have a special relevance to promoting the brand of an entire country, but they are equally applicable to companies which want to launch product or service brands in overseas markets.

Consumers, as I have already pointed out on several occasions, only devote minute amounts of their time to thinking about brands or the companies and countries which produce them, so it is essential that each one of these rare opportunities is used to maximum effect.

Having a clear, simple and distinctive brand strategy is the only way to ensure that each tiny message makes its own contribution to creating the desired effect in the consumer's mind.

3. **Leverage your people.** Every employee of the company (and, on the country level, every citizen of the state) is a potential communicator of brand, and therefore has a role to play in creating widespread opinion change. To overlook this essential fact is to ignore the cheapest and most effective advertising medium which any company or country can muster.

4. **Leverage your weaknesses.** Again, this is a point I will cover later, but it's worth remembering that consumer prejudice is not necessarily a bad thing: it can be more useful, for example, than complete ignorance of your company, product, or country. It is sometimes easier to turn a strong negative into a strong positive than it is to turn nothing into anything; consumer prejudice is a powerful force, and not easily altered.

5. **Leverage creativity.** Creativity is the most effective way of saving money that the marketing communications industry has ever discovered. In essence, it is about making your message so striking and unusual – yet relevant and believable – that consumers will *voluntarily* pay attention to it and remember it. There is almost nothing more expensive, or wasteful, than attempting to force large numbers of people to absorb a message which basically doesn't interest them. Creativity is the means by which communicators ensure that their messages are welcomed and recalled: the little dose of originality, humour, information, wisdom, emotion or shock is what leverages the *recipient* of the message into helping the communications process along.

   And creativity is not just about clever puns or striking images: as I mentioned earlier, the choice of communications medium is itself a creative opportunity. Putting a brilliant ad in the obvious media, alongside every competitor's brilliant ads, is the best way to limit the effect of that brilliance, whereas even a dull ad in a surprising or unexpected environment can work twice as hard as an award-winner. Playing by the rules is like driving down a road with high hedges.

6. **Leverage scarcity.** It is not usually wise to disguise the fact that a product is produced in small quantities, and scarcity itself can be a powerful attraction. If the consumer feels that he or she has had to make an effort to discover and obtain a product, this can add considerably to the product's brand equity. In other words, don't be a pushover.

7. **Leverage relevance.** A strong strategy enables a brand to profit from creating links to events which are already in the public mind – as quickly and decisively as such an approach demands. If, for

example, a relatively obscure country achieves sudden sporting success, or produces an international star, exporters need to be able to move quickly to associate their products with the temporary increase in public awareness of their homeland, and a clear strategy enables them to decide quickly and accurately whether the occasion suits the brand, or not.

8. **Leverage social change.** The brands which achieve the greatest success are those which, by accident or design, find themselves in the path of major social change. Nike, for example, is not such a major phenomenon simply because it spends so many millions on advertising, but because it managed to associate itself with sport and fitness in people's minds when following sport and being fit became a global obsession.

   Much of the art of brand strategy is, therefore, about the ability to put one's ear to the ground, like an Indian hunter, and hear when the bison are about to change direction and stampede in any particular direction.

9. **Leverage culture.** Marketing a product in another country cannot be done without a deep understanding of the basic cultural differences between country of origin and target market. There is always a balance to be created between the risk and attraction of something different which comes from far away, and the reassurance that it will perform as expected and satisfy expectations.

10. **Leverage the strength of your personality.** Consumers, on the whole, have more respect for brands which, like Diesel, appear to know exactly who they are, and don't try too hard to smooth down the rough edges of their personality. Many companies have wasted millions on attempting to project abject reflections of 'consumer desire', in the misguided belief that brand strategy and customer service are the same thing. They're not.

   Companies should beware the dulling effect of committees and conventional decision-making processes: what starts out with a fine intention to come up with the idea which everybody loves all too often ends up as a desperate, eleventh-hour muddle to come up with an idea that nobody minds.

11. **Leverage other people's media.** Buying space in commercial media channels is the obvious way to communicate a message, but it's also the most expensive: it's a little like renting a train to get from one city to another instead of simply buying a ticket. Riding on other people's media trains – using the endorsements of celebrities, associating with existing events or other brands, or linking the brand to what happens in the news – is always cheaper, and in the end it's more credible: people know that TV spots and magazine pages have been paid for by the advertiser and so, quite rightly, take the contents with a large pinch of salt.

Getting distribution and retail presence

There are various ways in which brand-owners can arrange to sell their products in a foreign country – by direct or indirect export, through a joint venture with another company, via a distributor or agent, licensing or franchising the brand to a local manufacturer or operator, even building or acquiring a manufacturing facility within the export market.

- However, since the model described in this book is based on exploiting the positive associations of the brand's country of origin, any arrangement which meant transferring manufacture to another country would risk reducing or negating this advantage. It would also take employment away from the country of origin, which rather defeats the object.
- Since many emerging-market exporters won't have unlimited funds available for overseas expansion, it's unlikely that an investment-related strategy, involving creating or acquiring a sole venture in the overseas market, would make economic sense at the beginning. It can, of course, provide a quick route to international expansion later on.
- Since the brands we're talking about are for the most part not well-established – at least not outside the home market – it might be difficult to strike any kind of licensing or franchise deal which would be to the advantage of the brand's original owner.
- For the purposes of this book, we are primarily concentrating on physical products rather than services, so there is little need, at least initially, to consider creating a branch or subsidiary in any export market. A sales office, on the other hand, even if it only contains one qualified individual – as the examples of Urvâshi and Techo show – can prove a very wise investment.
- The conclusion is that, in the majority of cases, a producer from a developing country wishing to build a brand abroad is probably looking initially at a direct export approach.

As we have seen, the traditional and to some extent unavoidable approach to direct export involves engaging agents or distributors in each overseas market, and handing over a share in revenues as well as a certain amount of control over the destiny of the product in return for the distributor's market expertise, and some reduction in the risk of the venture.

However, any arrangement which results in diminished control over the brand should immediately ring alarm bells for the exporter. By granting a distributor control over the positioning and promotion of the brand, there is a risk that the brand's personality might become distorted or misrepresented: this might cause the brand to underperform in the market, but an almost greater danger is that it will perform well, become established, and then create a far more intractable problem of incompatibility when a global positioning is developed for the brand.

For this reason, it is sometimes preferable to opt for agent-type rather than distributor-type relationships, even though it increases the costs, risks and responsibilities to the brand-owner, because it circumvents the problems associated with correct market representation. Once you've done a deal with a distributor, the brand effectively becomes his or hers, and this is not the best recipe for creating a coherent global brand. Owners of brands from emerging markets are unlikely to be in a position to be able to negotiate much control over the way in which their product is marketed once the distributor has taken delivery of it and paid for it; but all contracts can be negotiated, and it's certainly worth exploring all routes.

Unsurprisingly, most of the emerging-market entrepreneurs I meet tell tales of intense scepticism on the part of agents and distributors in developed countries when first exposed to the idea of helping to establish a new brand from a poorer country. It takes a visionary distributor to see the potential of such an initiative – a businessperson who is perhaps as courageous as the brand creators themselves. The default belief of any distributor or agent is likely to be that products from a developing country can only be cut-price alternatives to 'authentic' first-world brands, if not direct copies of them. So the discussion is likely to centre on price, and it takes some persuasiveness on the part of the brand-owner to help a distributor understand that not only should the brand be priced on a level with competing domestic and other first-world import brands, but might even command a premium.

Price, as all marketers know, is one of the most effective positioning tools in their armoury, as it's the one message which the consumer can't ignore. When there is any danger of a premium brand being perceived as a cut-price product, a somewhat inflated price might be the only means of dispelling this prejudice: it will certainly depress sales in the short term, but is a highly compelling way for a brand to draw attention to itself and communicate just who it thinks it is.

When Urvâshi was launched in Paris, Deepak pitched it at $130, which made it just about the most expensive perfume on the market at the time, and although this was considered an outrageous price for an unknown, third-world company with no history, no brand equity and no other product lines, it proved to be the right decision.

The temptation to price low is equally likely to be felt by the brand owner too: after all, one of the very few advantages of exporting from poor country to rich country is the favourable currency differential. A modest price-tag in a European market may seem ludicrously high to a producer from a South Asian country, for example, but it's crucial to evaluate every marketing message – price included – in the cultural context of the target market, or errors of judgment can easily be made.

Perhaps the most important article of faith for the producer of an emerging-market brand is that the distributor or agent is not, finally, the consumer, however important their expertise may be, and no matter how essential their role may be in achieving market access. In the end, what counts for the business is how consumers react to the brand and the way in which it is marketed.

Approaching a distributor or retailer already confidently armed with a mature and innovative brand strategy is essential: there's nothing like visible confidence in the potential of the brand for persuading a distributor that this brand is destined for success – along with fluency in telling its story, a clear vision of why and how it will appeal to consumers, and realistic plans about how the message can best be communicated. For this reason, any early help that the entrepreneur can get in developing and mapping out the international brand and communications strategy is worth its weight in gold. Later on, I'll talk about the value of 'seed marketing' as a crucial type of foreign aid.

However, probably the best means of convincing a distributor or retailer that a brand is worth launching in their market is to demonstrate in some way that consumers are already demanding it. Channel marketing, the process of persuading the distribution and retail channels to take on and show favour to a particular brand, usually presents a combination of data proving existing consumer demand, and examples of the planned consumer communications programmes which will stimulate and sustain ever greater demand.

While this is hard to achieve without a reasonable research and marketing budget, it's fair to say that almost any channel marketing isbetter than none, and a sincere and well-produced attempt to persuade the channel that the market has been analysed, that there's a fair chance that consumers will buy the product, and that there is a serious commitment on the part of the manufacturer to do whatever is possible to generate demand, will go a long way.

But if you want to steal petrol from a car, it's not enough to put a hose between one tank and another – you have to get hold of the receiving end and give a suck. In a similar way, it's often not enough to pour a product into the distribution and retail channel – only once the consumer starts sucking at the other end does the 'siphon effect' start to occur. So it's worth giving more thought to how consumer awareness and buzz can be generated before distributors are even approached; if nothing else, it puts the brand-owner in a stronger negotiating position.

Also, for certain categories of exporter – primarily, the owners of products or services which can be distributed entirely digitally like software, music, publications, banking or online consulting – the prospect of developing an international brand is much more accessible thanks to the internet, which enables exporters to circumvent the whole infuriating muddle and cut out the middleman. Even without a digitally-distributable product, the fact remains that all products are digitally marketable, so this allows unlimited brand control from the country of origin, at least in the interactive media.

Of course, making a product available isn't the same thing as selling it, and it's only realistic to assume that consumers in the developed world will feel anxious about making payments to, and expecting delivery from, an emerging country – in these cases, an association with a familiar and trusted intermediary brand for payment collection (e.g. Verisign, Digital River, Visa etc) and logistics (DHL, UPS etc) can make all the difference to a cautious consumer. Some of the trustworthiness of these brands will transfer, by association, onto the brand being sold: brands are also judged by the company they keep, and any opportunities to associate one's brand with trusted and established but non-competing brands with a similar positioning, ethic, personality or target market, should be seized.

All kinds of direct marketing are ways of circumventing the channel, but they are primarily a selling rather than a branding tool, and on their own they don't create quite as much brand value quite as quickly as the more emotive messages which appear in the mass media. There's still nothing like colour press ads, radio, posters and especially television or cinema commercials for attaching strong emotional values to a brand. So to achieve brand awareness as well as sales, and build it quickly, direct marketing is usually supported with a more conventional brand building campaign using paid-for media, or, if the budget is limited, at least an attempt to create word-of-mouth brand awareness through a viral or PR approach.

Having said this, consumer perception of a powerful brand is also powerfully influenced by the experience of dealing with the company that produces it – in an age of largely 'virtual' product benefits, this is one area where it's still very easy to distinguish a good company from a bad one – and another of the great liberations offered by the internet is that it enables a manufacturer to build a good and positive relationship with its customers at a distance, using an increasing range of interactive tools. Consumers will deduce a great deal about the quality and reliability of the products they buy on the basis of the quality and reliability of their transactions, before and after sale, with the company that makes them. It hardly needs emphasizing how difficult it is to achieve this quality of service, internet or no internet, from a distant market and an entirely different consumer culture.

It's also true that brands can be created 'organically' – through a long-standing relationship between a good product and a happy consumer – as well as 'artificially' – through the communication of brand values via marketing communications, so spending millions on pure brand-building exercises is neither sufficient nor invariably necessary for creating a powerful brand. Many would argue that the 'organic' route to brand-building is the surer and more robust approach, but it does require a good deal of patience, and markets move too fast for it to be practical in most cases.

Finally, as any good distributor or agent will be aware, the choice of retailer is an essential part of communicating brand values to the consumer, and getting placement in suitably upmarket retailers can go a long way to upgrade the image of emerging market products. Obviously, the competition for shelf-space in such outlets is intense, and as time passes, retailers tend to acquire more and more control and influence over manufacturers and brand-owners. This is partly because, just like using price to communicate value and prestige, the environment in which the consumer first encounters the brand – and where he or she has to go in order to obtain it – is in itself an incontrovertible marketing message.

Overseas marketing and branding

Earlier in this chapter, I described how consumers in undeveloped markets were relatively powerless when first confronted by highly sophisticated Western brands and marketing techniques: because in order to survive and prosper in the intensely competitive marketplaces of North America and Western Europe, those brands and their communications had already reached very high levels of subtlety and potency.

Conversely, a key challenge for any brand-owner from an emerging country is knowing how to market his or her brand in a way which will capture the attention of the jaded, message-fatigued Western consumer. On the whole, the kind of marketing which works back home in a less competitive environment will fail to attract much notice in a busier market, so there is every reason to assume that different executions as well as different strategies will be required.

However, there is a danger of over-reacting to this challenge and betraying the integrity, character and provenance of the brand by simply hiring a local advertising agency in the target country and teaching the brand to speak fluent OECD: we must assume that if the brand appeals in a Western market it is precisely because of its different and exotic origins, so the one thing our marketing probably *shouldn't* do is disguise or contradict its essential character, try to beat domestic brands at their own game, or worse still, pretend to be one: the most effective approach may even be a carefully-adapted variation of the original communications. This way, some of the true flavour of the brand's country of origin will be communicated to the consumer, and the fundamental cultural difference of the advertising approach will attract the attention of jaded consumers more effectively than any attempt to imitate the style to which they are already most accustomed to seeing, most adept at judging, and least likely to pay any attention to.

I raised the point in the 'Eleven Levers for Outsmarting the Competition' earlier in this chapter that consumers tend to respect and respond well to brands which seem to know who they are, and which appear easy and confident with their own identities. Such brands seem to be saying to the consumer 'this is what I am, and I'm proud of it – take me or leave me', and the approach, when it's well managed, seldom fails. There is a myth, frequently expressed by people who don't understand how marketing works, that selling a successful product is about 'giving people what they want'. In practice, the attempt to do so often fails, because we consumers often don't really know what we want until we see it.

The factor which works most powerfully in favour of global brands from emerging markets is their differentiation, which is impossible to imitate and difficult to ignore. It comes quite naturally to them, yet it's the one quality which Western brands struggle to achieve. No matter how sophisticated and attractive the products of an American or European or Japanese or Korean company may be, the one thing they can *never* be is Sri Lankan or South African or Peruvian or Latvian. It is this *differentness* on which, ultimately, their success will rest, so the absolute criterion for assessing every detail of distribution and marketing strategy and execution is this: does it respect, reflect and enhance the product's innate differentness, or not?

When marketing brands like these in difficult and highly competitive places, positioning is everything: where you place your brand in the marketplace – in what product category or sub-category, at what price, in which shops, and in the company of which other brands. This is the context which enables consumers to make the right judgments about its value for money and desirability, and will largely determine whether it succeeds or fails. The same product can often be positioned in several different ways, and each one will have important implications for the way in which it's sold and the number and type of people who buy it, and how much they're prepared to pay for it.

Roustam Tariko's Russki Standard vodka, for example, could have easily been positioned as a cut-price but authentic Russian vodka, and sold in supermarkets in the West at a relatively low price – 'the vodka which ordinary Russians drink' – and this positioning would have justified the low price and might even have created a certain chic. The high quality of the product would have come as a pleasant surprise to the consumer and generated valuable word of mouth publicity as well as repeat sales and customer loyalty. Promoting in this way would have meant a greater volume of sales, and the actual cost of manufacturing would have allowed fairly deep discounting, so the margins would have been tighter but there would have been more income to play with.

But Roustam had a hunch that there was greater potential amongst sophisticated urbanites in Europe and the US for a super-premium, authentic, heritage vodka brand – not Communist but Imperial – and that the right brand could command a substantial premium. What's more, the true story about Russki Standard's origins, as the only vodka to carry Tsar Nicholas' personal stamp of approval, gave the brand the *right* to compete with Smirnoff Black, Grey Goose, Finlandia and other premium-priced labels.

Defining and maintaining the personality of the brand, and defining and communicating the ideal positioning for it in an overseas market, needs a combination of expertise from the country of origin and from the target market, and there's no getting around this fact. The balance of influence and control between these two areas of expertise is crucial – too much control from either side can easily jeopardize the brand's chances of success. Possibly the best model is one where a trusted, country-of-origin individual or agency has the responsibility to partner with and collaborate closely with a near equivalent in the target market: for example, an advertising, PR, design, sales promotion or direct marketing agency from the home market which knows and understands the brand intimately, can take on the role of coordinating and supporting the work of an agency of similar size in each overseas target market.

A more controllable and more cost-effective solution might be to recruit a few talented individuals from the target market and bring them to work within the domestic agency, and although salary differentials between a developed country and the home market may make this solution look extravagant, it's likely to be cheaper in the long run than engaging full-service agencies in a distant country; and it brings control of the brand back home where it belongs. New teams can be added on whenever the product needs to be launched in a new country.[33]

Tariffs and other trade barriers

In Chapter 2, I mentioned how Brazil appears to have every condition in place to become a major exporter of branded products to the USA and other rich countries, and yet doesn't do so except in very rare cases.

One reason is undoubtedly that the U.S. and other rich countries appear to make it as difficult and expensive as possible for countries like Brazil to do so, through a bewildering range of quotas and non-tariff barriers which, without always flagrantly breaching WTO rules, are pure protectionism. Considering that the US is Brazil's principal trading partner, such trade barriers represent a crippling burden, and might partly explain Brazil's apparent preference for trading with its other South American neighbours and concentrating on building a regional power-base through Mercosur, the trade group of South American nations.

In a stinging report produced in 2001 by the Brazilian Embassy in Washington, the full extent of these barriers is catalogued in detail, and they are positively medieval in their complexity and pettifogging, mean-spirited, bureaucratic obstructionism. To demonstrate how unequal these barriers are, the Embassy compared the 15 main global export products from Brazil and from the United States. Based on 1999 data, the average tariff or tariff equivalent applied by Brazil on 15 US products was 14.3 per cent, while the average tariff applied by the US on the 15 Brazilian products was 45.6 per cent.

And remember that here we're only talking about commodities such as fruit juice, rubber, steel, sugar, coffee and textiles. Import duties on manufactured goods are significantly higher, much more so than the relatively lenient charges made to US companies which manufacture abroad.

In his 1994 book about Nike, *Just do It*, Donald Katz reported that Nike had to pay 'a whopping $5.90' in US Customs duty on every pair of Carnivore cross-training shoes as they arrived in the USA from the factory in Korea which produced them. This amounted to 4.5 per cent of the shoes' retail price of $130, which, if we are to believe him, was slightly more than the final profit which Nike actually made on each pair of shoes once all their overheads, suppliers and retailers had been paid. Most foreign companies – and especially poorer countries – trying to export to the US would be absolutely delighted if they only had to pay 4.5 per cent import duty on their products – in some cases it's closer to 50 per cent.

As Oxfam note in their 2002 report on global trade,[34]

> In their rhetoric, governments of rich countries constantly stress their commitment to poverty reduction. Yet the same governments use their trade policy to conduct what amounts to robbery against the world's poor. When developing countries export to rich-country markets, they face tariff barriers that are four times higher than those encountered by rich countries. Those barriers cost them $100bn a year – twice as much as they receive in aid.

The rich nations absolutely *love* to put their signatures to resolutions and edicts promising to 'eradicate world poverty', and 'end unfair trading practices which discriminate against the world's poor' because this is simply doing their PR for them. It gives them wonderfully quotable quotes which they can print in their Annual Reports and use against their detractors, secure in the knowledge that they are entirely unenforceable – and that as wealthy and privileged members of the elite groups which draw up such resolutions, they will never be called to account for breaching them. The only time rich countries *ever* chastise each other for breaches of such agreements is when they breach terms against each other: then the voices of protest become distinctly shrill.

The squabble about whether rich countries are more protectionist than poor, or vice versa, rumbles on. Some powerful arguments have been produced by Jagdish Bhagwati (amongst others), a professor of economics at Columbia University and an advisor to the WTO, claiming that protectionism is a more common characteristic of poorer countries and that, barring a few exceptions, the wealthier countries are on the whole conscientious free traders.[35] Bhagwati also shows that much of the worst protectionism in the modern world is between emerging nations. In the other camp – which is more vocal and often more persuasive – are such populist figures as Bono, as well as respected bodies like Oxfam and Christian Aid. It seems unlikely that either camp is entirely mistaken, and whether you're talking about North America or Central Africa, it is a rare politician indeed who is prepared to give international trade agreements priority over short-term domestic interests (and working-class votes).

Psychological barriers

One of the toughest problems facing emerging exporters has nothing to do with logistics or finance or marketing: it is simply doubts in the mind of the brand-owners about whether they're doing the right thing. And it's understandable: if you've grown up in a country where all the premium brands come from the North, it takes real vision and courage to believe that your own brand could be attractive enough not merely for consumers in your own country, but for the Northerners themselves to prefer it to the many American or European or Japanese alternatives available to them.

'The first thing is to convince yourself that you can do it,' Deepak Kanegaonkar says with a smile. 'That itself is very hard.'

Perhaps the most reassuring feeling in the face of these doubts is knowing, as I described earlier, that there actually *is* no alternative to your product from America or Europe or Japan, precisely because it doesn't come from any of those places: the brand is competing on its own terms.

For this reason, the emerging-market brands which are most likely to succeed abroad are the ones whose brand appeal depends in some compelling and ineradicable way on their country of origin. The relationship between the brand and the country it comes from will be explored in more detail in Chapter 5, but the basic principle is simply this:

- *unless* the manufacturer is absolutely certain that its product is innately superior to the products already available in the chosen export market

- *and* that this advantage is sustainable
- *or* it is committed to competing with local products on price alone
- *then* it shouldn't choose to compete with Western products whose benefits are primarily functional, or whose country of origin is immaterial within the sector.

The relevance of country of origin can, of course, be established by a newcomer in sectors where it has not previously been considered critical – usually because of a lack of choice: for example, until Royal Selangor appeared on the market in the United States, nobody thought it was particularly important where their pewter goods came from. Now, unless they come from Malaysia, those who are in the know consider them somewhat inferior. This fact has made life a great deal easier for Royal Selangor's competitors should they decide to export to America, which seems like bad news for Royal Selangor, but in the longer term it helps to establish the sector, and is definitely good news for the Malaysian economy.

Confidence also comes from knowing that there is a real consumer interest in your brand and its country of origin. This factor is explored in Chapter 6, which tracks the phenomenon of Western consumers' current infatuation with all things exotic – clearly, a significant circumstance for any exporter selling from East to West or South to North.

Confidence comes, too, from seeing others succeed, as I said at the beginning of the chapter. The real pioneers, like the ones whose stories I tell in this book, will give heart to those who follow in their footsteps; the bigger and more prominent players like Shanghai Tang, Škoda, Infosys, Embraer and Tata also give great reassurance – after all, even Nokia, the biggest brand in Europe and the world's No. 1 mobile phone brand, was once a new brand from an emerging market. As examples proliferate, so confidence will increase, and it should become a self-accelerating phenomenon: then, there is a real chance that major change will start to occur.

We should never underestimate the power of *chutzpah* – that indomitable self-confidence which has the power to simply steamroll the objections and doubts and hesitation of others in its way.

In the end, confidence is something that lies within each of us, just waiting for the right circumstances to emerge and give us strength. The daring which makes a tiny player want to attack a huge market, and really believe that it can succeed, is a kind of madness, and many stories of business success follow this pattern: at the beginning, a crazy visionary shows the way. Gradually, the amusement of others turns to admiration, and criticism mutates into a powerful desire to imitate. And then phenomenal change occurs.

What will become of our emerging market brands?

There seems little doubt that, if at all successful, the certain fate of our emerging market brands is that they will become acquisition targets for first world companies.

If some of them are bought out, this is obviously good news for the company owners, who will have the opportunity to realise the value on their businesses over a shorter period than would otherwise have been possible. For their home country, it's a mixed blessing, because even though the profits and the value of the company will pass into foreign hands, the chances are that the new owner will see the sense of maintaining the story of the brand's country of origin, so it will continue to act as an ambassador for the country. This effect may be much enhanced if the new owner can put more marketing muscle behind it and gain better distribution around the world: in effect, it lowers the barriers to entry for new brands from the country to follow the same path, as it gets across the message to consumers that these are products worth owning.

In this sense, for example, Amoy continues to promote Chinese cuisine, even though the company belongs to Danone; Škoda continues to promote positive Czech imagery and transfer the perception of high engineering standards onto other Czech brands even though the company is owned by Volkswagen.

In a sense, being bought out is the ultimate validation of an emerging brand-owner's success. If they are perceived by global companies to be a threat to an existing brand, or even acknowledged to have some kind of consumer appeal, then they have surely arrived.

The pioneers may get bought, but there are many camp followers.

Quality standards and consumer perceptions

Finally, we come to the question of quality in manufacturing and service provision.

Although quality standards and the consumer perception of quality are obviously very closely linked, quality isn't merely a matter of perception. As David Tang of Shanghai Tang says, 'of course it's not only the design and marketing skills that count, but absolutely ruthless quality control which is not yet fully appreciated in the second and third world – and indeed, the whole concept of making things that the open market actually wants'. Some producers in emerging markets, as we have seen, have benefited enormously from their experience of manufacturing on behalf of European and American brand-owners, and therefore the investment in quality systems has effectively been made for them; but those who have not enjoyed this advantage will need to achieve the same levels of quality in other ways.

Clearly, this issue should be high on the agenda of any emerging market government which understands the value of export trade. International accreditation bodies such as ISO have helped the situation by creating internationally-recognized benchmarks of quality processes so that the companies in developing countries know exactly what they are aiming for, and can be secure in the knowledge that their efforts will be recognized worldwide when they get there. The fact that some effort has been put into promoting these quality standards as consumer brands in their own right, which purchasers will look for and accept as guarantees of quality, is a most valuable development.

Quality control and quality processes are a big subject in their own right, and it's not within the scope of this book to cover the topic in detail. But if we assume that an emerging-market company can produce goods or services to 'international standards', then the most pressing issue is of perception rather than reality.

And this perception is intimately linked to the way in which the brand's country of origin is perceived by consumers around the world. Is it a country with a reputation for producing high-quality goods and services, or is it a country which people automatically associate with cheaply-produced, second rate stuff?

If it's the latter, it may be completely beyond the emerging exporter's powers to persuade overseas consumers that the brand he or she produces is worth owning, so powerful is the effect of an inappropriate or negative country of origin. This leaves producers with no choice but to conceal their actual provenance from consumers, or deliberately mislead them.

The most precious gift which a government can give to its exporters is a strong national reputation for producing quality products. As we have seen, such a reputation represents a powerful competitive advantage to producers who wish to acknowledge the origins of their brands.

Companies will, of course, need to pay their dues if they wish to enjoy the benefits of such a reputation – they will need to recognize their government as final arbiter on issues of brand, contribute to and comply with its strategy, collaborate with other companies and even competitors to promote the nation's reputation, and never miss an opportunity to acknowledge and promote their own products' country of origin. But there is no doubt that the 'team effort' can create major benefits to all parties.

This issue is central to the argument of global brands from emerging markets and needs to be covered in detail. I'll do this in the next chapter.

CHAPTER 5

When countries become brands

Why countries need brands

Any company in an emerging market which manages to overcome the obstacles described in the last chapter and export its products in branded form to another country – especially a richer country – can claim a major achievement.

If other companies are inspired by the success and kudos of these pioneers and decide to follow their example, then several things may start to happen:

- Some consumers in other countries may begin, little by little, to form an altered opinion about the country which produces these brands (assuming they know where they come from). Since the brand has communicated enough to them to make them notice it and pay money for it, they now have a tiny 'personal connection' with that country, and feel they know something about it. Some people who notice the products but don't even buy them may start thinking slightly differently about their country of origin.
- The people in the brand's home country, once they know how well a locally-made product is doing overseas, especially in richer countries, may start to feel a little more pride and confidence in their own status in the world. It's a little like knowing that your country's football team is playing in the World Cup.
- If the brand is also for sale in the domestic market, it may acquire a certain glamour as a result of its success abroad and even justify a price premium.

- It should become easier for the brand owner to attract high-quality employees when it becomes known that the firm's products are successful in other countries.
- The authorities in the country of origin may begin to realise the greater economic potential of such activities and start to think about encouraging more of the same.

But, as I said in Chapter 1, although some tangible and emotional benefits may spread out to the immediate environment of the exporting company, it's unlikely that really widespread changes in people's perceptions will occur spontaneously as a result of a few successful exports. For this to happen, government must seize the initiative, and undertake a comprehensive nation-branding programme around their best international brands, or around those domestic brands with the greatest international 'star potential'.

But when we talk about branding the nation, what exactly do we mean, and what is it supposed to achieve?

The question of a country's image has cropped up again and again during the previous chapters, and it's clear that countries (and, for that matter, cities and regions too) behave, in many ways, just like brands. They are perceived – rightly or wrongly – in certain ways by large groups of people at home and abroad; they are associated with certain qualities and characteristics. Those perceptions can have a significant impact on the way that overseas consumers view their products, and the way they behave towards those countries in sport, politics, trade and cultural matters; it will affect their propensity to visit or relocate or invest there; their willingness to partner with such countries in international affairs; and whether they are more likely to interpret the actions and behaviours of those countries in a positive or a negative light.

In short, the image of a country determines the way the world sees it and treats it.

This image may be entirely accurate and fully justified, but it is more likely to be at least partly untrue and unfair, based on a whole mess of misunderstandings, prejudices, cultural differences and half-forgotten events from history. Like any reputation, it needs looking after. Virtue and honesty are not always recognized in this world, and it's as important and as natural for countries as it is for people and products to want to be properly and fairly understood, and to ensure that the world is getting the right message.

The reason for this is simply that most people are much too busy worrying about themselves, their immediate friends and families and their own countries, to spend too long attempting to form complete, balanced, informed and unprejudiced views about six billion other people and two hundred other countries. We all tend to make do with a simple shorthand for the vast majority of people and places – the ones we will probably never know or visit – and only start to expand and refine these impressions when for some reason we acquire a particular interest in them.

When you haven't got time to read a book, you judge it by its cover.

If the leaders of a country decide that they would like more people to go beyond the common shorthand (perhaps because it's untrue or unflattering or unhelpful to their commercial or cultural or political aspirations), and form a fairer view of their country, then it's up to them to ensure that the right messages get across and people change their minds.

But the right messages alone can't make people suddenly decide to take a special interest in a distant country with which they have no particular connection: simply flooding the media with more true facts about a country is certainly ineffectual, possibly counter-productive, and in any case probably impossible.

It will be ineffectual, because people tend to be warmly attached to their prejudices: they are simple and convenient and probably compelling, and nobody has so much free space in their minds that they will voluntarily replace something short and memorable and interesting with a mass of loosely-related data which may lead to no single, coherent conclusion.

It may be counter-productive, because simply bringing a country to people's attention without changing their views about it will merely serve to refresh and reinforce their prejudices.

It will probably be impossible anyway, because the editors and journalists who decide what goes in the media understand extremely well what kind of information people like to consume, and they know that most of us have a very limited appetite for quantities of true, balanced, informative data.

Of course, you can spend lots of money and buy your own media space, but as I said in the last chapter, people long ago worked out that paid-for media space is simply a place where rich organizations can talk about themselves to their hearts' content, so it's often quite rightly ignored.

No, the only way to make people change their minds about things which don't immediately affect them is to make them *want* to change their minds – to offer to replace what they think with something so much more interesting and captivating, and yet equally portable, that they will happily oblige.

And that's called marketing.

Countries that change

One of the most dramatic examples of how a nation-brand can be dreamed up, communicated and established across much of the world is the case of Walter Scott and Scotland: Scott almost single-handedly defined the image of modern Scotland, right down to the tartan (the brand's corporate identity), the kilts, the bagpipes and the dialect.[36]

Much of his portrait of Scotland was highly idealized, some was a reinvention of long-forgotten cultural history, and parts were downright fantasy. Yet his novels portrayed a land so attractive, picturesque and compelling, it has remained rooted into the consciousness of Europe, and beyond, for centuries. The Scottish Tourist Board quite rightly plays on it to this day. It is a heartening example of how people can, if they are passionate and determined and gifted enough, sway the world's view of a nation; and it is one of the best examples of the power of literature to thrust an entire country into the realms of global iconography.

The best example of 'brand turnaround' from our own times is undoubtedly that of modern Japan, as we saw in Chapter 2. The effect of Japan's economic miracle on the image of the country itself was quite as dramatic as its effect on the country's output: 40 or even 30 years ago, 'Made in Japan' was a decidedly negative concept, as most Western consumers had based their perception of 'brand Japan' on their experience of shoddy, second-rate products flooding the marketplace. The products were cheap, certainly, but they were basically worthless. In many respects, the perception of Japan was much as China's has been in more recent years.

Yet Japan has now become enviably synonymous with advanced technology, manufacturing quality, competitive pricing, even of style and status. Japan, indeed, passes the best branding test of all: whether consumers are prepared to pay more money for functionally identical products, simply because of where they come from. It's fair to say that in the 1950's and 1960's, most Europeans and Americans would only buy Japanese products because they were significantly *cheaper* than a Western alternative; now, in certain very valuable market segments, such as consumer electronics, musical instruments and motor vehicles, Western consumers will consistently pay *more* for products manufactured by previously unknown brands, purely on the basis that they are perceived to be Japanese. Little wonder that Dixons, a UK retailer of consumer electronics, gave their new house brand a mock-Japanese name, Matsui, in order to borrow a little of the 'public domain' equity of Brand Japan.

And even as we watch, international perceptions of South Korea are quickly adapting to include the attributes of modernity, technical competence, manufacturing excellence, stylish design and ambition communicated by such brands as Samsung, Daewoo, Kia and LG; and the twin hosting of the football World Cup by Korea and Japan did much to confirm the sense that these two brands are of comparable stature.

Indeed, the branding of South Korea is already so far advanced that few people bother to specify 'South' Korea any longer when referring to the Republic. Just like West Germany before Unification, the richer country of the two, and not coincidentally also the producer of big international brands, is the one which automatically inherits the more powerful, simpler brand name (Germany or Korea), while the poor neighbour ends up with the cheaper sub-brand (East Germany or North Korea).

How the nation-brand helps branded exports

Go into a shop in any prosperous country – say, Germany, Japan or America – and you're faced with a wide range of branded products to choose from. Whether it's clothes, luxury goods, soft drinks, sports equipment, cosmetics, consumer electronics or household equipment, the variety is amazing.

Each brand competes for your attention by trying to offer something a little different from its rivals – sometimes the product itself is superior, sometimes it's designed in a more eye-catching way, and sometimes it's purely the name and the packaging and the advertising which makes the brand feel different, more attractive, more special.

But one thing's certain. Almost without exception, those brands come – or appear to come – from the same places: America, England, Scotland, France, Germany, Japan, Scandinavia, Switzerland, South Korea or Italy. These places are the Top Ten as far as brand image is concerned: tell people that a brand is made in one of these countries or regions, and they will immediately expect a certain kind of brand image, a certain level of quality, and be prepared to pay a certain price for it.

If Coca-Cola or Marlboro or Nike weren't American, if Ferrari or Gucci or Barilla weren't Italian, if Chanel or Dior weren't French and Burberry and Rolls-Royce weren't (originally) English, they would truly be half the brands they are today.

Of course, everyone knows that many of the products themselves are actually manufactured somewhere else, like China or Mexico or Thailand. This fact isn't usually mentioned in the advertising, which often borrows heavily on the image of the country where the company was started, or where it *sounds* as if it comes from, or where its worldwide headquarters are situated.

So German brands often present themselves as serious, solidly engineered and rather expensive, but worth spending a bit more on because they'll last practically forever and always work perfectly (they're probably also manufactured in Germany, which is part of the reason they're rather expensive). Somehow, even though most Japanese cameras are by now equal or superior to most German cameras in quality of manufacture, technological wizardry, style, price and ease of use, brands like

Leica still manage to retain a perceptual margin for themselves, a slight but apparently ineradicable brand 'edge' which is beyond practical considerations: in the end, a Leica is always slightly more desirable (even to Japanese consumers, apparently). An Italian brand will exude that effortless, sexy stylishness which no other country seems to be able to carry off quite as well. British brands often have snob appeal – old-fashioned, exclusive, traditional, hand-made, classy – and if you're in the market for that kind of lifestyle, there is simply no substitute.

More than any other country, America has been blessed with a huge range of positive brand attributes: one only has to observe its more successful export brands to see the expressive power of these attributes. America is associated with the definitive youth lifestyle (Coke, Pepsi, MTV, Levi's, Wrangler); with sporting prowess (Nike, O'Neill, Rockport, Reebok, NBA, Timberland, Champion USA), with technological supremacy (IBM, Compaq, Dell, Cisco, Palm, Hewlett-Packard, AT&T, Motorola, Intel, Microsoft); America is well-travelled (Boeing, Hertz, Marriott, Avis, NASA, Holiday Inn, Sheraton); well-informed (CNN, *Time, Newsweek, National Geographic,* NBC, Reuters); and, naturally, wealthy and powerful (American Express, Merrill Lynch, JP Morgan, Goldman Sachs, Forbes, Citibank, Diner's Club, Western Union). Coming from America even lends authority in areas which were once considered uniquely European, such as fashion (Calvin Klein, Donna Karan, Tommy Hilfiger, Ralph Lauren, The Gap), beauty (Elizabeth Arden, Revlon, Max Factor) and even food, albeit of the convenience variety (McDonalds, Pizza Hut, KFC, Taco Bell, etc.).

As we have seen, America also dominates the league tables of international brands, producing almost ten times the number of billion-dollar brands as its nearest rivals.

The core of America's potency is surely the fact that it is considered by most people to be the supreme country of origin for the world's three most valuable and profitable business sectors: entertainment, merchant banking and information technology. Its pre-eminence as a brand will probably only wane if it loses its 'ownership' of these three sectors, or if at some point in the distant future, they diminish in importance as drivers of global wealth and culture, and America is unable to stake an equal claim on their successors.

These and many other attributes make America, without doubt, the world's most powerful public domain brand. This may be merely one of the privileges of being a powerful and productive nation, but it is undoubtedly also the result of the fact that American has branded itself so competently as a country. The world's best advertising agency – Hollywood – has for nearly a century been pumping out 2-hour cinema commercials for Brand America, which consumers around the world have cheerfully paid to queue up in the rain and watch. Brand USA also employs such high-powered sales promotion agencies as NASA, which periodically launches a rocket into space, in order to communicate the superiority of American technology and manufacturing.

Consequently, American brands can simply hitch themselves onto this powerful national brand, and a cultural and commercial trail is instantly blazed for them around the world. Little wonder that so many brands from other countries are keen to borrow American attributes.[37]

Beyond America and the other 'Top Ten' country-brands, there are other places which have a certain appeal, although it's usually limited to one or two kinds of product or even a single brand: a brand from Australia that sends out masculine, humorous, outdoorsy vibes, or a funky Dutch product full of rebellious, youthful confidence. Countries like Ireland, Canada, New Zealand, Finland, Spain, Taiwan, Wales, Portugal and Belgium are minor country-brands in their own right, and communicate some things to some people – but, unlike the Top Ten, their appeal and their 'meaning' is less clear, or less powerful, or less global, and varies more from country to country. Most Germans, for example, will have a pretty clear idea what they would expect from a Belgian brand, even if they've never actually come across one before, but to the average Japanese, it would mean next to nothing. Likewise, Americans are fairly familiar with the idea of a Canadian brand, but once you get to Europe, people can hardly distinguish between the two (much to the exasperation of the Canadians).

The country images which so often guide our buying decisions are old, old clichés, and usually have little to do with the contemporary reality of the country. But like most clichés, there's probably a grain of truth in them somewhere, and they are so familiar that we accept them pretty much without hesitation. And because we believe in the country images, we also believe that products possess similar qualities to the countries they come from.

These little perceptual hints about the quality or nature of the product we're about to buy, although they only occupy a tiny fraction of our attention, are worth a great deal. Often, they are the first little push which gets the ball rolling, and creates a spark of interest or understanding in our minds about a particular product. At the critical first moment when a product appears in our field of attention, when the vast majority of products will need to be quickly eliminated if we are not to become seized up with too many brand names, a tiny hint of familiarity can mean the difference between selection and elimination.

It could be the vaguest, most fleeting thought – 'oh, it's from Slovenia, like those skis I bought last winter' – yet such a thought is of almost incalculable value to producers, because it gets their product *onto the shortlist*; it gets the brand out of the mass and into consideration; it makes it stand out from the crowd.

Then, of course, the product needs to be good and attractive and compellingly marketed if the interest is to be converted into a sale, but at least it's in the running and actually stands a chance of being evaluated.

The 'country of origin effect' is powerful and complex, and has been closely studied by marketers and academics during the last thirty or forty years – in fact, there have been no less than 766 major publications by 789 authors on the subject between the 1950s and 2001, according to Nicolas Papadopoulos, an academic at Carleton University in Ottawa who has made a special study of the field.[38] These books and academic papers, for the most part, analyse the way 'country of origin' works, the effect it has on the psychology of consumers, and how to harness it in marketing campaigns.

Marketing academics now worry a great deal about subtle distinctions between products which are *made* in certain countries, or *designed* there, or *assembled* there, and the effect that these differences have on the consumer's view of the product.[39] But on the whole, we don't really bother too much about where, exactly, American or Japanese or European products were manufactured or assembled, or where their original components were sourced, or whether the brand is now foreign-owned, because we feel that the 'home country' of the brand itself is what counts. This is our guarantee of quality or style or status, and the shorthand for a wide range of associations about the brand which make us feel good about owning it.

As I said earlier, consumers prefer to make informed buying decisions but they are short of time (and in the end, short of patience too: after all, even in the profoundly consumerist societies of Western Europe, the Far East or North America, people still don't want to spend *too* long worrying about products), and the country of origin of a product, just like a brand-name, is believed to be a short cut to an informed decision. If the information is too complex, we will simply discard any part of it which we feel is of secondary importance and revert to a simple belief: that's why most people, for example, still think of Range Rovers, Aston Martins, Rolls-Royces, Bentleys and Jaguars as being British cars, even though it is now pretty well known that they are all owned by German or American companies.

Perhaps the only time we think hard and consciously about country of origin, country of manufacture and country of brand, and take care to distinguish between them, is when we are intentionally buying ethically: in such cases, we are buying with our brains in gear rather than just following our instincts or emotions. When people buy FairTrade coffee, for example, they tend to read the packaging quite carefully for exact and truthful information about the product's country of origin, because such details form an important part of their decision to buy. This is a point I will return to in Chapter 6.

Most of the rest of the time, and quite understandably, we simply couldn't be less interested.

The case of Brand Brazil

I mentioned the case of Brazil in Chapter 2, and its near-total lack of any international brands, despite the very favourable circumstances of the domestic marketplace.

This lack is particularly striking when one considers that Brazil itself is surely one of the most powerful brands in the world. 'Brand Brazil' is packed with images which are consistently held by millions of consumers all over the world – ecstatic samba dancing at carnival time; the rainforests as endangered as they are exotic; sex, magic, beaches, sport, adventure, music, style, grace, *joie de vivre*. These attributes could be part of the brand print of almost any successful youth product on the market today, especially in food, sport, cosmetics, fashion, music and even cars. Brazil is the quintessential youth brand – it effortlessly elicits the range and type of associations in young people all over the planet which brands like Nike or Pepsi would do almost anything to achieve. It's hardly surprising that Nike thought it a worthwhile investment to sponsor the Brazilian national football team – literally buying a share in the equity of Brand Brazil – and equally understandable that the deal caused a great deal of unhappiness among Brazilians.

Certainly, some of the clichés of Brand Brazil may be depressing, even insulting, to the average Brazilian, but they are undeniably a fine platform on which to build a believable global brand. It is one of the tasks of a national branding programme to convert these clichés into something more creative, more substantial, more fair, more true; to take people's simple received notions and lead them towards a deeper understanding of the country's infinitely more complex and contradictory reality.

The fact that there are negative associations (pollution, overpopulation, poverty, crime, corruption) within the brand print of Brazil is far less of a problem in image terms than it is for the people who actually have to suffer the consequences of the problems. After all, a strong brand is a rich brand, and richness implies a complex and intriguing mix of many different elements. The brand equity of the United States also contains a significant proportion of negative elements, but this does little to diminish its attraction, especially if the audience you're dealing with is composed of younger consumers, whose prickly, contradictory nature means they demand to challenge and be challenged.

This kind of talk may sound callous, but it is important to understand that the existence of such problems, and people's awareness of them, is no reason for either the public or private sector to believe that the country's image is flawed and must therefore be changed or downplayed or kept separate from the country's exports. Of course the problems need to be addressed, and urgently; and the fact that they may not do significant harm to the prospects of exported products is no excuse for not committing the necessary resources to resolving them; but it would be a pity if worrying about the negative aspects of the country's image were to distract from the important task of generating more sustainable, high-margin export business.

People are often surprised to hear that there are no famous brands from Brazil, and reply that there *must* surely be some – such is the power of the country's own brand – but when asked to name one usually can't. In reality, the handful of 'Brazilian' brands which are to be found on sale in North America and Western Europe prove, under closer inspection, to be rather less Brazilian than they first appear.

Reef Brazil is a good example of this: a successful brand of beachwear, it is sold in more than 90 countries around the world. The company was actually founded by two Argentinean brothers in San Diego, California, and its only link to Brazil is that the founders used to go surfing there, and had their first pair of sandals manufactured by a Brazilian shoemaker. Presumably they felt that Brazil offered the American consumer more positive and exciting imagery than their own home country (the fact that the military regime in Argentina in the 1970's made surfing illegal may have played a part in this decision).

Reef Brazil's publicity material, including a calendar much prized by (male) surfers, features nothing but photographs of young women's bottoms. This image trades effectively on popular perceptions of Brazil – Copacabana Beach in Rio de Janeiro is famous for its daring bikinis – and these perceptions are also a very effective way of excusing it. There is no question that this kind of advertising would be lambasted as sexist and demeaning (which, frankly, it is) if it came from an American company, but Brazilians are allowed to indulge in such behaviour because of an odd cultural prejudice which accepts that, in their case, it's simply a harmless, healthy and amusing expression of Latin *joie de vivre:* it's sexy, not sexist.

Today, Reef Brazil describes itself in its publicity blurb as 'a company loyal to its roots and true to its beginnings', and like most multinational apparel brands, sources its products in a range of 'developing' markets, including Brazil. The bulk of the profits, presumably, go to the holding company, South Cone, Inc., of San Diego.

The fact that an American company would want to *pretend* to be Brazilian is a sure sign that there is potential consumer demand for branded products from Brazil, and that the brand image of the country is good enough for companies to think it worth stealing, but the Brazilian companies simply aren't there to meet this demand.

If Chapter 3 is our 'Hall of Fame' of international brands from emerging countries, then it's tempting to put the many brands which lie about their country of origin, like Reef Brazil, into a 'Hall of Shame'. But it would be churlish to criticize such a heart-warming story of poor immigrants made good, and even if the founders did come from Argentina and not from Brazil, that doesn't devalue their achievement.

Each case must be judged on its own merits, but in general it feels like a pretty low trick for successful companies in developed markets to steal brand equity – often the only competitive asset which a poor country might have – from developing countries in order to boost their own sales and give their products a different, more exotic feel.

The lesson in all this could hardly be clearer: the rich world has begun to recognize the value of emerging-market brand equity, and unless the rightful owners of this equity move quickly to stake their claim, it too will pass into the greedy hands of the rich countries.

What's wrong with where you're from?

If you ask them, most people agree that coming from countries like Germany, Italy, America or Japan adds credibility and appeal to products, while coming from a developing country – unless it's one of those rare exceptions, like Brazil, which happen to have a natural storehouse of positive imagery – is more likely to reduce a product's appeal. As we have seen, the perception is that companies in such countries don't manufacture to the same standards as companies in the North – they use shoddy materials and cheap labour, and the end product is inherently less valuable. With such thoughts in the consumer's mind, charging a premium price for such a brand becomes virtually impossible.

These prejudices are hard to fight, even though they contradict what the majority of consumers in the West already know: that most of the products bearing their most valued brand names are actually manufactured – to the standards which such brand-owners require – in poor countries.

We are left with a vicious circle: it's hard to sell a branded product for a high price if it is known to come from a country not perceived to produce high quality products; yet the country will never earn that reputation unless its brand-owners start telling consumers where they come from.

In one way, the corporations which own so many of the biggest global brands have already started the process of breaking this perceptual cycle, and certainly without meaning to, simply by acknowledging where they source their products. Over the last few decades, consumers have become very familiar with those humble little stickers on the underside of their American or European-branded toys and running shoes and domestic appliances ('Made in China', 'Made in Vietnam', 'Made in Thailand', 'Made in Mexico'), and they have quietly absorbed the fact that a great many of the products they buy are manufactured (to the high standards required by those American and European brand-owners, naturally) in poorer countries. As we have seen, it doesn't much affect their beliefs about the basic 'nationality' of the brand, but it is noticed, and remembered, as a separate fact.

The American and European brand-owners could hardly have done their supplier nations a better favour. This low-pressure public relations campaign on behalf of the emerging world has effectively communicated to hundreds of millions of consumers – with far more patience and subtlety than most global companies ever apply to the promotion of their own brands – the simple fact that most of the best products in the world are now manufactured in developing countries, thus neatly paving the way for manufacturers in those countries to start developing their own brands, and for people in the first world to buy them.

The perception only has to be enhanced a little further, and brought more explicitly to the consumer's attention, and another barrier preventing the development of global brands from emerging markets is removed.

Using 'country of origin' more creatively

It's clear that a home country with strong, positive and universally-recognized associations of trust, quality and integrity is a major advantage to its manufacturers as they face the harsh realities of global competition. In this respect, it's just like the way a new product from a well-known company is accepted by loyal consumers: the 'parent brand' stands in as a proxy for personal experience of the product, and encourages trial in a way which a new product from an unknown company can almost never do.

For a brand's home country to add this helpful dose of free additional equity, the product should 'chime' with its country of origin in the consumer's mind, and some kind of logic must link the two.

This logic may be simple or creative: in the case of manufactured brands, it could be the straightforward logic of category expertise which (for example) links Benckiser, a manufacturer of household cleaning products, with a new household cleaning product; or it could be the more lateral sort of logic which links Caterpillar, a manufacturer of bulldozers, with rugged footwear. In exactly the same way, brands from countries can range from simple national produce – pizza from Italy or soft drinks from America – to more unexpected but equally attractive pairings, like skis from Slovenia, clothing from Australia, or phones from Finland.

When you try to match provenance with product, there are some pairings that clearly make brand sense, and others that just don't. People might well buy Indian accountancy software (the debut of Infosys on NASDAQ has certainly helped this association) or even a stylish Lithuanian raincoat, and although I'm tempted to say that they probably wouldn't buy Peruvian modems or Croatian perfume, attitudes can and do change quickly. Fifteen years ago, who would have believed that Europeans could be happily consuming Tsingtao beer from China or Proton cars from Malaysia?

Only one thing is certain about the strange phenomenon which marketers reassuringly call 'consumer behaviour': predictions are more often wrong than right, and many great marketing successes have occurred as a consequence of an inspired or obstinate marketer choosing to ignore what consumer research identified as 'what consumers want.'

As any experienced researcher knows, research often tells us little more than what consumers have seen before, and what they find reassuring. As I said earlier, the simple fact is that we often don't *know* what we want until we see it for the first time, and part of the skill of the marketer is thinking of things which are unlike anything which any of us have ever seen before. Research is an essential part of learning about the market, helping to understand consumer needs and testing new approaches, but it is never a substitute for creativity, and is the worst possible tool for creating new products or services. The last person who can tell you what's the next big thing is the person who is actually going to buy it when it comes along.

When a country does have the courage, insight and creativity to move away from the classic paradigm of 'national produce' and celebrate the fact that it produces brands which make you think again about the country which produces them, the results can be far more noticeable, and consequently far more profitable. Somewhere in the mysterious processes of consumer logic (or perhaps 'logic' really isn't the right word for it), Caterpillar boots made sense, and the resulting brand extension benefits both the company's core business and the new business: it really is a case of two and two making five. There's nothing odd at all about Indian perfume (as I mentioned, it is actually a more conventional and long-established idea than French perfume); but Turkish shotguns or Slovene dishwashers are a more unusual idea, and Russian banking is a *really* stimulating challenge to one's preconceptions.

Changing a country's brand image

Changing the world's perceptions of a nation is neither easy nor quick – after all, its brand image may have evolved over many centuries, shaped by wars, religion, diplomacy or the lack of it, international sporting triumphs or disasters, famous and infamous sons and daughters, and latterly, of course, by the brands it exports, as long as the brands are prepared to be explicit about their country of origin.

A nation-brand is like the proverbial supertanker, which takes five miles to change course and eight miles to stop. In many cases, all that the 'managers' of the nation brand can realistically hope to do is identify and isolate the positive existing perceptions of the country and calculate how to enhance whatever contributes to these in the country's external communications, while downplaying anything which doesn't.

The logic behind this approach is, as I said at the beginning of this chapter, standard marketing practice: the country is competing for consumer attention alongside a million other phenomena in the media, and unless its every appearance in the public domain continually and accurately reinforces a few simple, coherent and compelling truths, it is highly unlikely that a clear image will ever form itself in the consumer's mind.

In this respect, brands are rather like those children's games where you have to join up the dots to draw the outline of an animal – unless the game is made pretty easy for the consumer (i.e. the dots are numbered) – then he or she is unlikely ever to make out the tiger and might easily end up with a three-legged bunny or a lopsided house.

In reality, it takes *enormous* patience and wisdom to broadcast a few simple perceptions about a place, and help them to take hold on public consciousness around the world. There are almost no short cuts to this process: one simply has to determine the appropriate brand strategy, and then find ways to galvanize every single organization, individual, action and production of the country into reinforcing that strategy.

Some gestures are undoubtedly more effective and lasting than others. Jonathan Griffin, when he was Chief Executive of the UK's public diplomacy body, Britain Abroad, noted that there is a spectrum of public diplomacy activities which countries typically practise, and these can be graded according to the speed of pay-off they offer to the country's image, and the depth and longevity of the relationships they help to create with target audiences and other countries: on the 'slow' side of the spectrum are the strategic, long-term, deep, relationship-building activities like government scholarships and exchange programmes; at the opposite end are instant messaging, news management and crisis management.

As a rule, events which take place suddenly, however dramatic they are, and however radical the shift in perception they create, are relatively short-lived, whereas changes which take place over a longer period of time also tend to stay in people's minds for longer.

So a country which wins the World Cup can enjoy a dramatically enhanced reputation for sporting prowess – and all the positive attributes that go with this – but it seldom lasts even for the four years until the next competition, unless the country works very hard to capitalize on the improved reputation and build it into something more solid. Countries which consistently perform well over many years – like Russia in athletics or Brazil in football – will find that the positive perception is more durable, and may survive through several years of relatively poor performance.

Coordinating the messages given out by a country is like that school physics experiment where you hold a magnet under a sheet of paper covered with iron filings: the filings just form a random heap until the moment the magnet is in place, when they miraculously align themselves into a perfect and predictable shape around the poles of the invisible magnet. A strategy is the magnet; the iron filings are the thousands of messages which every city, region or country constantly sends out into the world – through advertising (for products and services, for inward investment, for trade and tourism), through acts of policy, through cultural exchange, through the diaspora and the people at home, through sport, through literature and films, through embassies and consulates, through trade relations and through millions of every-day business and social contacts (Figure 5.1).

Often, there is no need to increase the number of those messages or change the means by which they are communicated: it's a common misconception amongst countries trying to manage their reputations for the first time that they will have to raise tens or hundreds of millions of dollars to fund a global 'campaign' of some sort in order to communicate the new messages. As I have shown, people are in any case somewhat sceptical of obviously paid-for messages, and whilst image-building campaigns certainly have their place in a properly thought-out brand strategy, just as much can often be achieved simply by *aligning the existing communications* to a properly worked-out strategy, than by adding yet more new messages to the mix.

The term 'public diplomacy' was first used by the United States Information Agency in the early 1960s, in an attempt to communicate

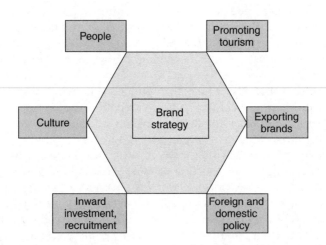

Figure 5.1   The National Brand Hexagon

what is meant when a modern state manages its reputation abroad.[40] The full definition of the term at the time was:

> 'the influence of public attitudes on the formation and execution of foreign policies. It encompasses dimensions of international relations beyond traditional diplomacy; the cultivation by governments of public opinion in other countries; the interaction of private groups and interests in one country with those of another; the reporting of foreign affairs and its impact on policy; communication between those whose job is communication, as between diplomats and foreign correspondents; and the processes of inter-cultural communications'.

In my view, the concept becomes fully useful only when by 'public' we refer to both the mouthpiece *and* the recipient of the message. Country branding occurs when public speaks to public; when a substantial proportion of the population of the country – not just the civil servants and paid figureheads – gets behind the strategy and lives it out in their everyday dealings with the outside world.

When the entire population is galvanized into becoming the mouthpiece of a country's values and qualities, *then* you have an advertising medium which is actually equal to the enormous task of communicating something so complex to so many.

And we've all seen this approach in action, even if we've seldom seen it done consistently or thoroughly. How often, for example, have we completely changed our minds about a country simply because of one good friend who comes from there, or one clever business associate? That single plain-clothes ambassador has effected a complete and possibly permanent conversion of one 'consumer' in favour of the 'brand' which he or she represents. The ultimate aim towards which nation branding should aspire is creating such a sense of pride and purpose that the entire population begins, almost by instinct, to perform such acts of conversion, every day of their lives: an impossible target to attain, of course, but the direction in which one should strive could not be clearer.

It's true that each individual 'branding' action, and its effect on the whole world's perceptions of the country, may seem heartbreakingly tiny, hardly even worth doing: a mere drop in the ocean.

But the ocean is made of drops, and what is truly heartbreaking is when thousands of people, companies, products, politicians, personalities and cultural artefacts are drop-drop-dropping messages every single day about their country and it doesn't amount to anything, because there's no method behind it, no guidance, no strategy, no vision, no common purpose.

As I have said, some actions are more effective than others, and the words and deeds of a well-known person are many times more potent than those of ordinary members of the public: because famous people are under constant observation by millions of other people, their actions and preferences have enormous leverage.

When, for example, Madonna decided to buy a house in London, this probably communicated more effectively, and to a larger number of people, that London was a 'happening' city than a year's worth of ordinary tourism promotion. And the main reason it was so effective was because it was a real news event, taking place in the real world: it wasn't created inside the artificial and simulated world of paid-for media. A real person had made a real decision about her own life, and millions of Madonna fans around the world decided that, if they had the money, London was where *they* would buy a home too.

Such events automatically receive major coverage in the world's media, which is free publicity for all concerned – the kind of promotion which, if it had to be paid for, would probably have blown the London Tourist Board's annual budget in one go.

As I mentioned in the 'Eleven Levers of Outsmarting the Competition', one of the key skills of marketing on a limited budget is learning how to hitch a ride on somebody else's media train rather than going to the trouble and expense of making your own and keeping it running: when a country wins the world cup or even simply qualifies, it is riding free on the massive media train which world cup football powers; when Madonna buys property in London, then London rides on her media train.

Such events might, at first glance, just look like good luck: but as everyone knows, luck is something you make. A country pursuing a national branding programme can, if it wants, spend huge amounts of money simply publishing its strategic wish-list in the world's media, or else it can try to help luck along and make good things happen.

One of the best ways to make your own luck is by practising what I call 'hand of God marketing'. This is not marketing in its commonly accepted sense: it means working entirely behind the scenes, scouting out which people, brands and events create the biggest and most positive leverage effects on worldwide public opinion, and doing whatever is possible and legal to ensure that those people and brands and events publicly demonstrate their attachment and approval and loyalty to your country.

The technique is just like curling, that quaint old Scottish sport, where you spend most of your time frantically brushing the ice in front of your 'rock' with a broom, smoothing its path towards the destination you choose, without ever actually touching it.

Some circumstances, are, of course, entirely beyond a country's control, and may cause sudden, dramatic and lasting changes in perceptions. If the country is embroiled in a war, a natural disaster or a scandal, then media attention will ensure that the event gets free, instant and worldwide coverage, and it quickly becomes almost impossible to control the effects of it. It is arguably one of the benign effects of the globalization of media that governments may now think somewhat longer and harder before behaving badly; a greater awareness of the importance of the national brand and a deeper understanding of its principles may cause them to consider more carefully what such an action could do to their reputation, and consequently to their trading, financial, political, cultural and other relationships.

I mentioned before that when companies brand their products, they are entering into a two-way pact of trust with the consumer, which places them in the limelight, and should ultimately compel them to behave more benignly, transparently and accountably than otherwise. The same is equally true of countries. There is nothing like the discipline of branding to make one realize the true value of a good reputation, and to teach one to respect and protect it above all else.

The corollary of this phenomenon is, of course, that media attention will be paid in similar measure to any individual or group which is prepared to do something newsworthy: the 'brand equity' of a terrorist group or mass murderer can attain, briefly, the same levels as that of a legitimate state. And since, unlike states, such factions or individuals care nothing about their good name, they may gain access to unlimited global publicity for a short time. This brief blaze of glory may sometimes be one of the main reasons why the atrocities are committed in the first place: unfortunately, we can't enjoy the benign influence of global media without occasionally submitting to its counterpart.

What's in a name?

Perhaps the most extreme cases of country re-branding are those where a place has actually changed its name. As commercial branding teaches, this is one of the riskiest exercises which one can undertake: in throwing away the old name, one is throwing away the container of brand equity, and thus, almost inevitably, the equity which it contains. Clearly, this is not a decision to be taken lightly, and it is generally only justified when the old name is doing so much damage to the world's perceptions of the country that to continue to use it is positively harmful.

It is seldom the right thing to do when it simply reflects the desire of the current administration to 'update', 'refresh' or 'revise' people's outdated, jaded or indifferent views of the country, or perhaps because the country's existing name is somewhat similar to the name of another country, and they don't want people to confuse the two.

Governments sometimes worry a bit too much about the name of their country, and forget that what really counts is what you make it stand for.

The only way to refresh a country's image is for it to do refreshing things, and communicate those things tirelessly and imaginatively around the world: in other words, to change the contents of the vessel, not throw away the vessel. People need something in which to hold their perceptions, and a familiar name is usually the only means they have for doing this. Perceptions cannot exist for long without a container or a context – especially when you consider what a very tiny proportion of his or her day the average person dedicates to thinking about foreign countries.

Similarly, the way to stop people confusing your country with another country is not by changing its name, but by changing its behaviour. One anonymous place can easily be mistaken for another, but it is less likely that people will confuse a prominent and successful country with one that's less famous, even if they do have similar names: Britain and Bhutan sound rather similar, and so do Ireland and Iceland, but people don't get them muddled up half as often as they do with Slovenia and Slovakia, or Niger and Nigeria.

(It's interesting that the most successful country brand of them all manages to pull off the ultimate branding trick and sustain *two* equally powerful and entirely equivalent brand names without causing any confusion whatsoever: just as 'Coca-Cola' and 'Coke' both point to the same brand, so do 'America' and 'The United States'.)

But names are in some ways surprisingly unimportant. Fame and reputation have a trick of investing even a boring or wrong-sounding name with a special resonance in people's minds, which makes them gradually less and less aware of the word's particular characteristics. As I mentioned in my last book, most British consumers are convinced that the American food brand, Heinz, is 100 per cent British, because they have been familiar with it for so long, and have simply cancelled from their minds the fact that it sounds 100 per cent German. Likewise, 'James' is an extremely common Anglo-Saxon first name and 'Brown' an equally common surname; yet 'James Brown' is undeniably more than the sum of its rather unpromising parts.

Paradoxically, it's the smaller and less well known countries which are most likely to want to change their names and are also the least likely to be able to pull it off. Big and successful countries, like big brands, might well succeed in transferring their reputation more or less intact from one brand name to another, for the simple reason that their name is constantly on people's lips, and people will have plenty of opportunities to practise and get accustomed to a new version of it.

A small brand, or a small country, which doesn't occupy very much space in the audience's attention, is much more likely to disappear without trace if it ditches the only part of itself with which its audience is remotely familiar.

If people think anything about your country at all, you're very lucky, because it means that you register on their radar screens, you *exist*, and there is a basis of knowledge or belief that you can work from. There is no doubt that it's much harder work to start a ball rolling from standstill than to change its direction.

Chris Powell, Chairman of the UK-based National Endowment for Science, Technology and the Arts, tells how the government of New Zealand decided to embark on a campaign to improve the image of their country, and asked a colleague of his to carry out research around the world to see what people thought of New Zealand: 'He concluded that they didn't.'[41]

And if that knowledge or belief which people hold about your country is inappropriate or outdated, the one thing you shouldn't do is try to contradict it. People don't take kindly to being told that what they have believed for a very long time is wrong. Martial arts teaches that if a heavy opponent is charging towards you, the last thing you should do is try to stop him in his tracks, as he will surely flatten you: you should leverage his forward momentum in order to encourage him to proceed in the direction *you* choose. It is thus with perceptions: as I said earlier, take the clichés and the commonplaces, and turn them, over time, into something truer, richer, and fairer.

You sound like you're from ...

Brands like Matsui from Britain, or Bossini and Giordano fashions from Hong Kong, which steal their homeland from a better-established place in order to augment their natural brand equities, are common enough, and have been around for a very long time. The existence of such 'cuckoo brands', as I call them, also serves to emphasize the enormous power of language in the context of building international brands.

It is a great asset for a country to have a language which people around the world can instantly identify, even when they are looking at unfamiliar names, perhaps even when transliterated into a different writing-system. This makes 'decoding' the country of origin of a simpler, faster and more efficient process. People around the world are so familiar with the 'music' of Japanese or Italian or English names, for example, that they can instantly identify their supposed country of origin, even when the names are entirely made up, like Bossini or Matsui.

Sometimes this effect is achieved deliberately, and sometimes not: the fact that so many people quite spontaneously take Nokia to be a Japanese rather than a Finnish name may have done much to ease the brand's acceptance; but the very German-sounding brand name Haier, adopted by the Chinese refrigerator company I described in Chapter 3, was deliberately chosen in order to make the brand more acceptable in export markets. Indeed, Akio Morita's decision in 1954 to give the Tokyo Tsuchin Kogyo company the Latin-based name 'Sony' was avowedly to give the company's products a more international relevance; it might equally have been to disguise their Japanese origins.

It has long been observed by academics in marketing and linguistics that the sounds of brand names not only appear to make direct communications about the nature of the product represented, but they also trigger cultural stereotypes.[42] In one study, products with French-sounding names were invariably identified by American consumers as 'more hedonistic' than when they were presented with English-sounding names.

In other countries, English is, unsurprisingly, the language most commonly hijacked in the cause of added brand value. All over the world, wherever American or British attributes are considered attractive by consumers, there are English-sounding products for sale, many of which sound laughably contrived to native English speakers, but which communicate a world of imaginary glamour, quality, style and heritage (or youthfulness, street credibility and modernity) to millions of consumers.

Marketing consultants Al and Laura Ries report visiting a Tel-Aviv shopping mall and noticing five stores in a row with the following names: Gold Shop, Happy Tie, Happytime, Royalty, and Make Up Forever.[43] My last book contains a large collection of similar absurdities.[44]

Another fine example is Ronhill cigarettes from Croatia, which is clearly a blend of two well-known English brand names, Rothmans and Dunhill. This is one of many examples of brands which not only steal equity from somebody else's country but also from somebody else's brand: the latter is against the law; the former is not.

At least not yet. In an age where countries are beginning to invest huge sums in shaping and promoting their brand equities, one cannot help wondering how long pilfering of national identities will be tolerated. Perhaps the Italian region of Tuscany's announcement that it would take steps to protect its 'natural imagery' from copyright theft (it seems that two-thirds of all car ads, for example, are shot in Tuscany, no matter which country the car is made in), will prove to be the first of many.

After English, Italian is probably the language most frequently usurped by foreign brand owners. With Italian, it's the endings which make it easy to synthesise instantly-recognisable names: you just add an 'azzo' or an 'etto', an 'ello' or an 'ino' to a word and you have instant Italian appeal. The American company Pizza Hut, for example, once launched a kind of pizza pie called the *priazzo*, a word which has absolutely no meaning to an Italian speaker, apart from sounding vaguely offensive: but to the American public, it had instant connotations of authentic, hand-made, tasty, old-world Italian quality.

All that rich, 'value-added' communication from four letters stuck on the end of a rather inelegant made-up name: it's not surprising that country-of-origin effect is so prized by brand owners.

The difficulty is when your language simply isn't familiar enough to consumers in other countries for them to identify your brand's country of origin simply from the phonetic characteristics of its name – Finnish being a case in point, as the example of Nokia well illustrates.

This linguistic-recognition factor certainly adds another facet to the argument for the commercial benefits of promoting a nation's language and culture to the outside world, a subject to which I will return in the next chapter.

Slogans, shorthand and the nature of the country brand

As people frequently and quite rightly point out, a country is not a product, and while there is huge potential in the enlightened, imaginative and responsible application of product marketing techniques to places, it is certainly not the case that countries may be dealt with as if they were soap powder.

Perhaps the first rule of branding a country is to be acutely conscious of the limits of what one can and should achieve by it. It's safest to treat 'brand' as nothing more than a metaphor for a country: many of the tricks and techniques of product marketing, as we have seen, provide useful parallels for how governments can get their messages across. But once you start believing that your country (or your political party, for that matter) really is nothing more than a product which needs to be targeted at a demographic, you are heading for trouble.

A more accurate and more useful metaphor than 'country as product brand' is 'country as corporate brand' – in other words, instead of drawing parallels between the country itself and product brands like Dove or Snickers, one considers it as something more like a holding company which manages a group of related sub-brands: a Unilever or a Mars.

In some ways it is even more revealing to draw parallels between countries and ingredient brands like Lycra, Nutrasweet or Intel. So rather than 'enveloping' the product (which is probably a more natural way of looking at it), the 'country of origin effect' is considered as a component of each product brand exported from the country. Just like a Lycra or Nutrasweet or Intel, the country brand is a statement of constant and dependable value (in other words, a short cut to an informed buying decision) which can be shared by any number of 'host' brands which are exported from the country. The country brand envelops them all in a kind of 'family', and grants each of them some of its lustre, yet without compromising the essential competitiveness or unique personality of any one of them. Thus, 'Made in America' functions in a slightly different way depending on whether it's acting as an ingredient of the Coca-Cola or Pepsi or Microsoft brands; each is free to be itself, but each is also immediately recognizable as a member of the 'Made in America' family of products.

One advantage of seeing country brands as an ingredient is that they no longer need to embrace and overarch the entire range of products and brands which a country produces: they simply add 'a little something' to each one. This makes arriving at a usably concise definition of the country's essence a rather simpler matter – indeed, that 'little something' might be a quality which can be expressed in a single word.

Thus, the ingredient brand called Italy adds sexiness to product brands. France adds chic. Germany adds integrity. Britain adds originality. And, if consumers are also prepared to believe it, why not say that India adds generosity, Thailand endeavour, Slovenia creativity, China wisdom, Russia daring, Sri Lanka intelligence, and Brazil youth?

One could argue indefinitely about whether these particular words are the right ones, but reducing the national branding component of exported products to a single word is neither a trivializing nor pointless exercise, since the simplicity required of the brand essence increases in direct proportion to the complexity of the task and the size of the country, the number of communication channels, and so forth. In a start-up company, where one only has to depend on a handful of people to communicate a brand, one could arguably get away with quite a complex brand strategy, because ensuring that each employee fully understands the strategy and how to apply it is a relatively small task. But even very small countries have thousands of communicators and communication channels (and, unlike most companies, the vast majority of them are completely uncontrollable), so the simpler the message, the better chance there is of getting people to take it on board. People need a simple guide to behaviour: and the simpler the better.

The paradox of how to turn something very rich and complex into something simple and memorable without diminishing its richness and complexity is at the heart of all mass communications. It's also the main reason why more than half of all the countries developing their brand strategy at any given moment are quite likely to come up with the positioning 'land of contrasts', which is really a tourism slogan (and not a very good one either).

It's important to remember that branding a country is not at all the same thing as promoting tourism: tourism is just a part of the whole. In fact, the image presented by the tourist industry is quite often irrelevant, unhelpful or even damaging to the country's other international initiatives, especially promoting for trade or inward investment. A typical example of this dissonance was faced by both Scotland and Ireland when they were working on their national brand strategies: both countries enjoyed an extremely valuable tourist image based on wild, empty countryside, quaint old-world charm, and a populace widely perceived as warm-hearted, uncomplicated, old-fashioned, rustic and utterly unsophisticated – hardly a useful image to have lodged in the minds of

American or Japanese corporations deciding where to build their newest semiconductor plant.

One resolution to this particular problem comes simply from the observation that whether you're talking about tourism or FDI, a key issue is still whether the country is a nice place to be or not: semiconductor plant workers as well as senior management need to like the place they are expected to live in: what they are looking for, and what the average holiday-maker is looking for, aren't in the end so very different. It's all about standards of life.

Such contrasts and contradictions, for the very reason that they exist in the real world, can be resolved, harmonized and believably communicated in a country's branding programme. It takes creativity, objectivity, branding sense, and a deep understanding of the way in which consumer logic works – or can be encouraged to work – in each target country and each target audience.

Quite simply, countries are contradictory, and one has to deal with this. Most people appear to have little trouble holding complex and even contradictory views about countries: as Mark Leonard points out, it is not unusual for young Muslims to revile America while acknowledging, almost in the same breath, that their fondest wish is to go there to study, live and work.

The definition of brand as shorthand or signpost for value, or quality, or equity, is a useful one: in other words, you don't attempt to pack all meaning into a single proposition or slogan, or jump the gun on the time it takes for a consumer to 'learn' the complex product, but be content with a sign which can stand for, and later refer accurately back to, the whole experience, once it is more familiar to the consumer. One has to have the wisdom and patience to accept that this sign will not be wholly meaningful to the consumer at the start, but it is a vessel which will become more and more replete with meaning as meaning is absorbed.

Most 'country slogans' are in fact the sad result of a committee's attempt to keep everyone happy by packing several conflicting agendas into a single statement, and it's not surprising they often end up sounding so bland. As Doug Lansky reports,[45] many countries use somewhat similar slogans:

> These are slogans that could, without exception, be used to describe every country, state, province, city, and town on the planet with only minimal exaggeration. Singapore has 'So Easy to Enjoy'; Mauritius has 'Fascination'; and Poland's 'The Natural Choice' could even apply to a fruit drink or high-fiber breakfast cereal. Switzerland went for the very clever 'Your Holiday', while neighbor Austria kicked in with 'Holiday Breakaway.' Turkey has 'Welcome to Friends'; North Carolina has 'A Better Place to Be' (better than what? The Ethiopian/Eritrean border?); and both Iceland and Thailand share the single word 'Amazing' (Zimbabwe used to be

'Amazing' as well, but recently changed). Fort Worth's was a little confusing: 'Capturing the World's Attention'. (Are they planning a terrorist strike soon?) Texas has 'A Whole Other Country'. (Apparently they've seceded from the Union without telling anyone.) Colombia's is 'The Continent Country'. I asked what that meant and they said, 'It's like a whole continent in one country'. Detroit abandoned 'Expect a Lot' (I guess expectations got a bit too high) for 'It's a Great Time'.

Simplification has a tendency to reduce appeal, since so much of the ultimate appeal of a country is its richness and complexity. The true art of branding is distillation: the art of extracting the concentrated essence of something complex, so that its complexity can always be extracted back out of the distillate, but it remains portable and easily memorable. The distillate, rather than actually attempting to contain all the detail of the country in question, is simply the common thread, the genetic constant, which underlies the basic commonality between the different parts of the brand.

Good image, bad image

When companies and countries are in trouble, people are often heard to lament the fact that bad news seems to travel so much faster and further than good. One spends years painstakingly attempting to create a positive image of a product or of a country, and often with barely discernible progress; yet the moment there's a silly scandal or a rumour of trouble, it goes round the world in hours and makes the front pages without any difficulty at all.

It seems unfair, but it's entirely to be expected. People always prefer the unvarnished truth to the 'official' version, and while the positive messages about a company or a country might possibly be the truth, they might also be lies, whereas the belief is that any messages which a company or country really doesn't want you to hear can *only* be the truth.

Britain had a particularly bad year in 2001: its livestock was infected by a nasty bout of foot and mouth disease, causing its beef to be banned from many export markets and many rural areas closed to tourism; and this followed just a few years after revelations that some British beef was contaminated with the infamous 'mad cow' disease, which had apparently caused several deaths. Then came the September 11th hijackings, and the all-important American visitors decided, understandably, to stop flying for a while.

Research carried by the British Tourism Authority late in the year suggested that foot and mouth disease was as well-known and well-covered by the media in America and Western Europe as any major brand. In fact, in terms of its unprompted awareness, foot and mouth was briefly a slightly bigger brand than Coca-Cola, which costs about a billion dollars a year to maintain, and despite the fact that the British Government had spent quite considerable sums in attempting to *prevent* this particular phenomenon from becoming famous.

Companies (and, to a degree, countries as well) often use their brands as glossy, impenetrable shields which they hold out to the consumer in order to mask the confusion, muddle, inefficiency and perhaps worse which lies behind. It only takes the merest hint that a chink has opened in this armour, and reality has poked its ugly face through the gap, and absolutely no marketing budget is required to promote it; indeed, no amount of money or influence can prevent people from *dragging* out what they believe to be the truth.

Not only do bad events travel further and faster, they also survive longer in people's memories. Countries commonly suffer from what I call the 'starlight effect', an image in people's minds which is based on the still-resonating memory of long-past events.

These effects are extraordinarily difficult to deal with, but one can learn valuable lessons from observing the ways that bad news works, and the peculiar hold which it has over people's imaginations. There is a way of telling positive truths about a country which borrows from the style and 'grammar' of editorial and is far more persuasive than the old-fashioned 'perfect world' school of marketing communications which may have made sense in the 1950's but seldom cuts much ice today (such is the majority of tourism advertising, which is often the closest a country gets to 'advertising itself' in a literal sense).

Sometimes all it takes is a few rough edges, a more balanced tone of voice, a less bland and condescending way of addressing the consumer, and a more discerning use of traditional advertising media.

The task may seem, as I mentioned before, enormous and unassailable, but especially when one is dealing with urgent perceptual change, it's worth bearing in mind that countries seldom need to target the entire world at once – it will almost always be possible to identify key countries and key opinion-makers within those countries, and concentrate on them.

These approaches are well worth adopting even when you're not dealing with bad stuff. Prevention is better than cure: despite the perception that bad news travels faster than good and erases all one's good work in an instant, it isn't really so. A carefully built up positive equity will stand a country in extremely good stead should something negative occur, and do much to insulate the country's reputation from severe harm, as well as ensure a speed recovery.

Country brands do sometimes become tarnished, and a long-term commitment to a proper recovery strategy, covering both actions and perceptions, becomes essential. In such cases, it's important to distinguish between country brands which are perceived as 'culpably' tarnished and those which are 'pitiably' tarnished: it is a good deal harder to convert general opprobrium into approval than pity.

The dilemma of control

Once a country's brand image begins to improve, a virtuous circle comes into play: the country promotes the brands and the brands promote the country. Branded goods promote tourism, tourism brings real income; foreign policy promotes inward investment, which improves the environment for branded exports, which sustain the country image, which improves tourism, which makes consumers more receptive to representations of culture, which stimulates the purchase of branded exports, which encourages more producers to export their brands . . . and so forth.

But none of this will ever take off in a big way if it's done piecemeal. The initiative has to be a major, nationwide, public-private partnership. The government, tourist boards, airlines, major brands and corporations have to agree on a common branding strategy (informed by a profound understanding and objective evaluation of overseas markets), and stick to it for many years.

Ideally, a government department needs to be established with this exclusive mandate, and fully empowered to make it happen. It is this department's job to drive the strategy forwards, create standards, ensure compliance, and generally commit itself to making sure that every single message which comes out of the country – whether it comes through exported brands, tourism promotion, inward investment or employment promotion, art, culture and sport, acts of foreign policy or the comments of internationally-renowned personalities – plays unerringly on the same basic themes.

In the commercial sector, it is openly acknowledged that a certain heavy-handedness on the part of brand managers has usually proved essential in order to achieve the kind of ruthless adherence to strategy and sticking on message which companies need.

There is, in fact, little that is democratic in the way that most companies are run, and powerful brands are often the result of a very single-minded, even mildly deranged, 'visionary' simply eliminating anybody who dares to deviate from the company line. To a degree, this is comprehensible: so much of the success of any branding venture is attributable to the amount of consistency which the company manages to achieve in its internal and external communications, that a somewhat despotic management style is often found to be the simplest way to achieve this. In a company, it is also permissible to some degree, since one supposes that the employees are there of their own free will, and are being paid to perform in a way which the management decides is in the best interest of the company.

Countries, obviously, are different. A manager in a company may be ruthlessly single-minded and this can benefit the company enormously; the same approach by the leader of a country is called tyranny and seldom achieves positive results.

And yet one knows from experience that getting many independent people and organizations (all with very different interests, opinions and agendas) to speak with a single voice is a hard thing to achieve through consensus. I am no student of political science and leave it to others to tackle the problem, but one thing is clear: unless a government can find a way of achieving in its committees the same single-minded sense of purpose and control which the crazy brand visionary achieves within a privately-owned company, nothing will come of the national brand programme, and it is doomed to fail.

Having said this, it's important not to get too carried away by the notion of adherence to brand values and create a compliance dictatorship. There will always be justifiable exceptions to the rules: for example, it's not invariably appropriate or desirable for brands to stress their country of origin. In Chapter 3, I quoted Dilip Kapur, the president of Hidesign, questioning the importance of provenance, even in a luxury goods sector: he asked, 'Why does a brand need to come from somewhere?' – and it's a perfectly valid question. Many companies in emerging markets tend to have a quite deeply-rooted reluctance to trumpet what they see as their humble origins, and there's no point in trying to bully them out of this mindset. It is, nonetheless, important to distinguish between disguised ineligibility syndrome and a fair, objective strategic appraisal of what's actually right for the brand. This is, at heart, a cultural issue: prejudice against one's own country of origin and in favour of wealthy nations is often so deeply rooted as to appear like common sense.

Although it will hold up the country-branding initiative, it's perfectly acceptable and probably inevitable that some brands made in countries with no image or a negative image will at first camouflage their origins, or even pretend (as many have done in the past) that they come from America or Europe. But over time, the greatest potential for them and for the brands which follow them will come from an explicit acknowledgement of their provenance, and its relevance to their brand values.

As corporations acquire more and more power in society, the proper role of government alongside them needs to be reframed. It seems likely that managing the national brand and coordinating its promotion and communications will continue to be a key role for government, as it has always been, despite some changes in the vocabulary used to describe these responsibilities. The indifference of an elected government to *individual* commercial interests continues to be its primary and irreducible qualification for playing this role; for the same reason, it is best fitted for the job of curbing the growing power of corporations, and negotiating hard on the funding of sensitive cultural and social areas (such as education) so that business gives as much money and retains as little influence as possible in these areas.

I've also mentioned, in the context of encouraging the growth of high-margin export businesses, that government has a responsibility to recognize, educate and nurture creative and business talent while also luring back the talent which has gone abroad. Creating the best possible environment for sustainable and profitable global companies to launch and flourish within the home market is key; and ensuring that the profits of these businesses benefit the wider community is not only in the interest of the country as a whole, but, as I will show in the next chapter, likely to do the businesses a favour too by ensuring that their 'stories' are as ethical, transparent and appealing as possible to increasingly concerned overseas consumers.

The importance of objectivity

Of all the qualities needed by those who are responsible for nurturing a country's image, objectivity is one of the most valuable, and one of the hardest to achieve. After all, the people responsible for marketing a product are generally salaried employees, are seldom the inventor or manufacturer of the product, and so don't find it too difficult to take a cool, objective view of the brand they're building: indeed, good Marketing Directors are prized partly because of their ability to see the brand through the eyes of the consumer.

But when the product doesn't come out of a factory, but is the homeland of the people trying to market it – where they and their parents and grandparents were born, raised and schooled – when they are public servants rather than marketing professionals, and when branding easily becomes confused with foreign policy, tourism or trade promotion, objectivity becomes an extremely elusive quality.

A lack of objectivity can be fatal to the proper branding of a country, no matter how good the intentions at the start. Typically, a country branding program will start with communications ministries and public affairs departments producing lists of their country's achievements and natural advantages: the nation's most distinguished sons and daughters, the role it has played in world events, its own major historical moments, gems of architecture and natural beauty, regional cuisine, language and folklore, all served up with pages of indigestible demographics and statistics about GDP and income per capita. The idea is that this mass of data is then distilled into a pithy slogan and a raft of quasi-tourism collateral, and thus the country is marketed to a waiting world.

From the point of view of a busy consumer halfway across the world, of course, the historical achievements and natural advantages of most countries are of little interest, and seldom add up to anything which could be described as a coherent or powerful brand. Indeed, since branding programmes are most urgently needed by the smaller, poorer and newer countries, it is all the more likely that such facts will make pretty unimpressive reading to the detached observer. On more than one occasion, I have been faced with the tricky task of gently explaining to a very proud and very patriotic minister that the world will not be enthralled by the fact that the world's first all-metal suspension bridge was invented by a man whose grandfather came from his country, or that over sixty different species of wild grass grow along his eastern coastline.

I know of no better metaphor for any marketing task than trying to chat up someone in a crowded bar. In effect, you walk up to somebody whom you've never met, and have a few seconds in which to convince them that you are worth getting to know better. Sometimes, a joke will do the trick, but if the bar is in Finland or Iraq (unlikely), where making strangers laugh is tricky or frowned upon, a different opening gambit might be preferable. Either way, there are few countries and few people who will fall in love with a stranger who kicks off the conversation with a long list of his natural advantages, impressive family tree and key achievements.

Anybody who doesn't like the sound of this either doesn't like reality, or doesn't like people.

No, the place to start working out how to brand a country is not with the country itself, but with the consumer and the marketplace. In the limited amount of mindspace which each consumer has available to store perceptions of foreign countries, one must identify where there are gaps and where there are opportunities. Is there room for a country which is the ultimate youth brand? Which country could most credibly seize this opportunity? Which country is best suited to become the ultimate downshifter's paradise? Which country could position itself as the next technological minipower? Which could be the most natural source country in the world for alternative dietary and medicinal brands? Where might the best service businesses in the world be built?

Brands as vectors of national image[46]

Branding has a deep responsibility in this changing world, which is closely connected with its role in promoting nation-states, regions and cities: whether we like it or not, commercial brands are increasingly performing the role of transmitting national culture.

We know that it's valuable for branded products to talk about their national identity to consumers; and increasingly, brands are actually the means by which those consumers form their views about national identity in the first place. While an older audience might associate Switzerland, for example, with William Tell (culture), cheese, chocolate, cuckoo-clocks and banking (unbranded produce and services), mountains and skiing (tourism), or neutrality (foreign policy), the first associations of younger people are far more likely to be Swatch or Swiss Army (branded products). Similarly, the first reaction of most children when asked what they know about Japan is 'Sony', 'Nintendo', 'Hello Kitty', 'Sailor Moon' or 'Pokémon'.

One commercial consequence of such brand-informed images is that they tend to stereotype countries in a two-dimensional way which makes it harder for exporters of 'non-typical' products to gain acceptance in overseas markets. For example, Italy's brand image as a fashion and style producer made it very difficult for Olivetti, a computer manufacturer, to create a successful export business; German fashion brands like Hugo Boss and Jil Sander have always downplayed their national origins, because fashion products don't chime with the consumer perception of a rational and technical Germany generated and sustained by brands like Bosch, Siemens, Porsche, AEG, BMW and Mercedes.

But this is a relatively minor problem, and it's hardly beyond the wit of a competent marketing organization to get around it: the real risk is that this convenient shorthand gets in the way of a deeper understanding of a country's cultural output.

As brands gradually become the dominant channel of communication for national identity, it becomes ever more vital to push the other channels – by encouraging first-hand experience of the country via tourism, by the careful management of international perceptions of a nation's foreign policy decisions, and by the representation of national culture.

To create a fair, rounded and attractive picture of a country in people's minds, a balance needs to be maintained between the different elements. The more successful country brands, like the United States, have always taken care to ensure that other channels of cultural and political communication (the United States Information Agency, Hollywood, the Voice Of America, etc.) have filled in the gaps around the brands (Coke, Disney, Pepsi, Levi's, Nike, Marlboro, etc.).

And as we have seen, the image which a country projects to the world will also have its effect on the population of the country itself: just as corporate branding campaigns, if properly done, can have a dramatic effect on the morale, team spirit and sense of purpose of the company's own employees, so a proper national branding campaign can unite a nation in a common sense of purpose and national pride. (If badly done, it can prove exceedingly divisive).

It follows that if the inhabitants of a country see that their civic and cultural achievements are recognized abroad, this will help to create a more productive cultural environment, whereas if the country is perceived as nothing much more than a factory, producing cars or toys or designer fashions, then the people involved in cultural pursuits may start to be considered less 'useful'; they may even start to *feel* less useful. Engineering and business studies will become more popular than the arts and humanities, funding will be easier to find for businesses than for cultural initiatives, and so forth: it's a vicious circle, and when the arts become underfunded, the quality, dynamism and creativity of business and industry suffer as a direct consequence.

The Macdonald Royal Commission in Canada came to a similar conclusion in 1985:

> There is, then, another aspect to culture, namely good taste, good design and creative innovation, that should enable smaller industrial economies to compete effectively in the world economy ... In this endeavour, higher quality implies an organic relationship between business and engineering, on the one hand, and design and craftsmanship, on the other ... High-quality products, technologies, plants, homes, cities and locales require the presence of creative artists of all kinds. To increase the long-run supply of artists ... governments must support the artists and the arts. The long-term return from investment in artists and the arts is real and substantial. In the absence of strong public support of this sector, Canada will not reap these benefits. Governments at all levels should increase their contribution to their respective arts councils.[47]

It does sometimes seem as if globalization is turning the world into a gigantic supermarket, where nations are nothing more than products on the shelf, frantically trying to attract the attention of each passing consumer. It's because no thinking economist, politician, manufacturer or consumer could possibly want to live in a supermarket that we have to turn our attention to all the sources of competitive advantage, and find irreducible roles for culture and humanism within the limits of the dominant economic system.

Not all forms of competition in a single world are a zero-sum game, and whether we are talking of culture or commerce, one country's win doesn't only come about through another country's loss. It is always more helpful to speak about a nation's contribution to global culture, rather than how successfully it promotes its own cultural interests.

In a world dominated by the capitalist system, it's easy to conclude that real competitive advantage can only come from economic strength. However, as in any busy marketplace, there is room on the global stage for brands which play by slightly different rules; there is room for niche brands, and room for brands which compete primarily on cultural excellence, rather than on economic muscle. Haiti, for example, may have difficulty attracting tourists, but its primary source of income is the export of naïve art, an industry which has suddenly found access to global markets through the internet. Haiti is still the poorest country in the Americas, but a niche market may prove the beginning of a useful specialist cluster.

The importance of representing culture

The role of culture in promoting a country is quite often thought of as problematic: people acknowledge that there is clearly some kind of requirement to represent the cultural attainments of a country, but there is a concern that they don't 'sell' – or provide return on investment – in the same way that inward investment, brands or tourism do. So culture becomes relegated to the status of a 'not for profit' activity, a kind of charitable or philanthropic obligation.

But to see representing culture as an obligation is to misunderstand its power to communicate a country's true spirit and essence. In truth, culture plays an essential role in the process of enriching a country's brand image, in driving the process from the initial shorthand of media communications towards a fuller and more durable understanding of the country and its values.

Culture uniquely provides this extra dimension because, in the face of the consumer's suspicion of commercial messages, culture is self-evidently 'not for sale:' to use a cynical metaphor, it's a 'promotional gift' that comes with the commercial nation brand. Culture is, if you like, the rich harmonic accompaniment to the simple, accessible, easily memorable melody of commercial competitive advantage. You can whistle a country's commercial brand, and not its cultural counterpoint; but the former is worth very much less without the latter.

Another of the values of culture in national branding is that each culture, like geography, is a truly unique feature of its country. Once you start looking at features and benefits, in classic marketing style, you are inevitably driven into common and non-unique territory, and one country starts to resemble another. A typical example of this trap is the tourism campaign which, by selling the feature of blue sea and sky with sandy beaches and the user benefit of relaxation and a golden tan, makes all seaside destinations indistinguishable from each other.

Representation of a country's culture provides the country's image with that all-important quality of dignity which, arguably, commercial brands can do without, but countries cannot. The Western consumer's knowledge of Japanese art, poetry, cuisine and philosophy, for example, however shallow it might be, functions as an important counterpoint to the commercial image of Japan: productivity, miniaturisation, technology etc. It helps to reduce the potentially threatening image of a highly, even aggressively efficient producer nation, by reassuring consumers that they are buying goods manufactured by real human beings, not automata. And Japanese pop culture provides the counterpart to the 'no fun' perception which might otherwise prevail, while also feeding imagery – and hence added attraction – directly into exported products. This process is common to almost all representations of pop culture, which are by definition closely linked to the commercial aspects of national promotion.

In a similar way, the strong and widespread perception of Germany as the home of great classical music, literature and philosophy, has helped to provide an extra human dimension to the sterile, brand-generated and ultimately copiable image of Germany as a mere factory producing expensive, highly functional and rather over-engineered consumer products.

Brand Italy manages the same kind of balance: if Italy's image was only communicated through its commercial brands, which are mainly in the fashion and lifestyle arena, it might seem like a shallow, super-ficial, fun-loving and highly stylish place but without much depth; so the high awareness of figures like Michelangelo, Dante, Leonardo, Galileo, Vivaldi and Verdi (not to mention Luciano Pavarotti, Roberto Benigni and Andrea Bocelli in more recent times and in a more popu-list vein) as well as the 'location sub-brands' of Venice, Florence and Rome, provide a profound counterpoint to a very attractive melody.

The challenge for all countries is to find ways of continually presenting and re-presenting their past cultural achievements alongside their modern equivalents in ways that are fresh, relevant and appeal-ing to younger audiences. This task is made ever more complex by the increasing plurality of modern societies – to celebrate the glories of a typically somewhat monocultural past without marginalizing or seem-ing to ignore the multi-racial reality of the country's modern-day popu-lation is a real quandary for most countries. Still, since the only solution is to give equal emphasis to present-day cultural enterprise, it is basically a productive dilemma, because it lessens the temptation for countries to rest on their laurels and live in the past.

Unless a country can build its culture as a body of understanding – a powerful brand – in the mind of its worldwide audience, then it faces a daunting and costly process of constantly re-establishing its right to be noticed and remembered.

In the mind of the consumer, culture also works in many different ways as a metaphor for personality, and people deduce a great deal about the inner qualities of a nation through its cultural enterprises. Sport equals strength, courage, physical prowess, agility, determina-tion, team spirit, honour, fair play, and so on. Pop music equals street credibility, flexibility, creativity, imagination, a sense of fun.

The cultural aspect of national image is irreplaceable and uncopi-able because it is uniquely linked to the country itself; it is reassuring because it links the country's past with its present; it is enriching because it deals with non-commercial activities; and it is dignifying because it shows the spiritual and intellectual qualities of the country's people and institutions.

Culture is a more eloquent communicator of national image than commercial brands, even if it does work more slowly. Brands in any case will always have their own commercial imperatives, and will, quite rightly, only comply with the official country branding strategy as long as it helps their sales. By contrast, the communication of culture can be pretty much agenda-free, as it is mercifully not answerable to the tyranny of Return on Investment, and its stakeholders usually ask for nothing more onerous than fair and truthful representation.

Culture as a revenue earner

Culture isn't, of course, an invariably unprofitable activity which always needs external funding in order to exist. Many cultural activities, often but not always in the area of popular and youth culture, are profitable and marketable products in their own right. National and international cultural events like concerts, exhibitions, competitions and festivals – even circuses, as Cirque du Soleil shows in the contribution it makes to the popular image of Canada abroad – can enrich the perception of a country while paying their own way.

Conversely, not all acts of commercial marketing are worthless as representations of culture – as I have mentioned before, the marketing of youth products tends to go hand-in-hand with the dissemination of popular culture, and some products even function as highly efficient communicators of 'classical' culture. Urvâshi, as we saw in Chapter 3, purveys a little Hindu culture with each bottle; and some Mont Blanc pens are currently carrying a promotion which celebrates the genius of Mozart (although it has to be said that this originally German company with a French name currently owned by a Swiss corporation embraces not only Austrian composers, but is associated with artists and musicians from a wide range of countries – the net effect is a European brand representing European culture).

Like Mont Blanc, many businesses also view sponsoring cultural events as the ideal means for promoting their own status as cultured, philanthropic, intelligent and cosmopolitan corporate citizens.

Any disciplines where art and business meet have the potential to be effective carriers of cultural messages – for example, the 'creative industries', like graphic, product and packaging design, advertising, music videos, web design, television and radio production, magazine and book publishing – and even though their purpose isn't high culture but the application of creative skills towards a commercial end, they are just as effective in deepening and dignifying the brand print of the country. The fact that Britain, for example, is known to produce witty and occasionally beautiful TV commercials, speaks volumes about the quality and creativity of the national environment, and helps in its own way to encourage inward employment, investment and probably even tourism. The way a brand is sold can be as important as the brand itself in communicating something of the country which produced it.

Promotional messages about certain aspects of the national brand like, say, tourism or 'ways of life', are often more readily believed and accepted when the channel of communication is itself a cultural artefact, rather than paid-for media. For example, experience suggests that good quality travel writing often has greater and more durable impact as a promoter of tourism than conventional advertising, and certain films tend to achieve the secondary effect of promoting their locations almost as a matter of course. The effectiveness of these channels is partly due to the fact that consumers are, as I have mentioned, so adept at recognizing – and discarding – paid-for promotional messages, and will naturally give more credence to objective, third-party endorsement through independent editorial or literary comment; and it's partly because the use of rich, cultural channels of expression carries its own authority and persuasiveness, which classic advertising, given its commercial and time/space constraints, can rarely achieve.

And language, the primary means of communicating culture, is an important ambassador of culture outside the home country – there is no more direct, durable, profound or agreeable way of learning a culture than by learning its language, as the success and popularity of the British Council overseas clearly demonstrates. Here, it must be said, some countries are luckier than others – the English-speaking nations are blessed with the advantage of being able to purvey the most sought-after language on the planet at this time.

Still, at least in the developed world, our increased leisure time, greater disposable income, more and more frequent international travel, and a growing trend towards lifelong learning, mean that more and more languages should become marketable exports in their own right.

Why representing culture is central to nation branding

I've spoken about how representing and promoting culture is an essential component of enriching the nation brand, and how, over time, it alone has the power to turn simple clichés into something more fair, something believable, something rooted in truth and history: something humanist, instead of the synthetic, two-dimensional commercial definition of 'brand' that we are accustomed to in the world of shopping.

But we can't avoid the question: why try to brand the nation at all? Aren't the available channels of commercial communication simply too narrow to admit the passage of something as rich and complex as culture or heritage? Isn't marketing a country and its culture simply a recipe for cheapness, the acquisition of superficial gloss at the expense of real texture, real learning, real thought?

I believe that we have little choice in the matter. Because, as I described earlier, so much of the wealth of nations in the globalized economy derives from each country's ability to export branded goods, and because so much of the wealth to survive and prosper now comes from the 'added value' of branded goods and services, the competitivity of nations and the branding of countries is the only way forward; it has become an immutable law of global capitalism. Adding culture and heritage to the mix is simply one way to ensure that all conversation between countries doesn't descend into mere advertising, and that there is still cultural exchange on a global scale, intelligent dialogue, sharing of insights and learning.

And in the end, whether we like it or not, the international promotion of each country's culture is essential for the renewal and regeneration of culture. Demand must be created for culture as for products, according to the rules of the global marketplace, or else supply will be threatened. Indirectly too, competition and economic growth must be pursued, because, whether we like it or not, the story of great culture is most often told against the background of stable, wealthy, well-ordered mercantile societies.

Finally, all countries have their own contribution to make to the world's store of culture, and thus all countries have an equal interest – duty, even – to add their voice to the chorus. If they fail to do this, then we all run the risk of ending up with a lopsided, impoverished and etiolated form of global knowledge.

Most people understand that the idea of cultural purity is false, and all culture is the result of a complex mixture of many different influences. I dispute that any individual nation's culture, however pervasive, however 'commercial' or 'superficial,' is actually pernicious, but it does need balancing. There can be no intrinsic harm in, for example, a consumer in India being exposed to 'brand culture' from America and Western Europe, as cultural influences are always absorbed, adopted, adapted, personalized or rejected in an entirely natural and 'democratic' way, just as foreign loanwords are adopted, adapted or rejected by other languages.

But if the trade-winds of cultural influence start to blow too regularly in the same direction, and cultural exchange becomes cultural colonization, then we all run the risk of handing down an impoverished global culture to our children and grandchildren.

Ensuring that a nation's culture is properly recognized as a vital channel of self-expression, as a vital component of its brand image, and thus a vital part of its opportunity to create sustainable prosperity, is the start of this process, which ultimately leads to an understanding that all nations have a shared responsibility to engage in cultural exchange. As so often happens, what begins as an act of competition is soon revealed to be an act of teamwork, and essential for the common good.

Further benefits of a strong national brand

As we have seen in this chapter, a strong national brand brings many advantages.

Paul Temporal, in an article on the need for Asian countries to brand themselves,[48] lists the following benefits which accrue from having a robust and positive national brand image:

- Increase currency stability
- Help restore international credibility and investor confidence
- Reverse international ratings downgrades
- Increase international political influence
- Lead to export growth of branded products and services
- Increase inbound tourism and investment
- Stimulate stronger international partnerships
- Enhance nation building (confidence, pride, harmony, ambition, national resolve)
- Reverse negative thoughts about environmental and human rights issues
- Help diffuse allegations of corruption and cronyism
- Bring greater access to global markets
- Lead to an improvement in the ability to win against regional and global business competitors, and defend their own markets.

One could produce a list of benefits that is four times longer than this without being excessively fanciful.

John Pantzalis and Carl A. Rodrigues[49] have even proposed that the movement of international capital is influenced by perceptions of countries as brands by investors. They claim that positioning and managing the country-brand are critical in attracting global capital, and affect how and when capital may flee a country in situations such as the 1997 Asian economic crisis. It's certainly a striking thought – that apparently hard-headed investors may form their view of a country's economic prospects as a result of the way in which that country's brand image has been presented to them in the media, or that they might class several countries together because of superficial brand associations (e.g. the 'Asian Tigers'), rather than anything more scientific.

We have begun to see how developing and pursuing a national brand strategy can encourage more moderate and benign foreign policy, because it concentrates the minds of political leaders on the real importance of their international reputation. If ordinary citizens are made to feel instrumental in shaping and realizing the international aspirations of the country, this may help to create a stronger sense of national identity and promote social inclusion, by uniting the whole country in an objective examination of its strengths and weaknesses, and undertaking a very open and public process of focus and improvement.

Clearly, there's far more to a powerful nation-brand image than simply boosting branded exports around the world. If we pursue the thought to its logical conclusion, a country's brand image can profoundly shape its economic, cultural and political destiny, for the simple reason that even global policy-makers are partly ruled by their heads and partly by their hearts. What ultimately makes the European Commission decide which countries will be considered for membership of their élite club, and in which order? Consciously or not, their deliberations also relate to the brand image of each applicant state, and what it might or might not ultimately contribute to the brand image of the Union itself. When complex wars erupt between countries, and even experts are hard-pressed to say which is truly the victim and which the aggressor, it is surely the brand image of each country that sways world opinion towards its customary black-and-white view. And when suspects are tried by international courts for acts of terrorism or espionage, public opinion (and almost certainly the judge and jury too) are unfailingly swayed by their brand of origin.

A positive brand image can help a country to reverse the 'brain drain': one of the consequences of globalization which is hardest on emerging markets is the haemorrhaging of its best-educated and most talented workers, entrepreneurs and academics to the developed nations. But the sense that these individuals could be part of the process which makes their own home country a land of opportunity is often enough to lure them back home.

As Lars Gellerstad puts it,[50]

The opportunity which branding offers new and developing nations is great indeed. It gives them a tool to focus away from the Socialist notion of relative power coming from 'tonnage' – tons of steel, barrels of oil, pounds of gold, bushels of wheat, bags of cocoa. It liberates them from the prison of having the land owners (their clan leaders) own the country. The view is still free; the air is for everyone, and a Brand Image is shared and built collectively. It is a great unifying project. In the past, such projects fell to the writers of the history books, searching back in time for great deeds and tales to inspire the populace – like William Tell – but (re-)branding looks forward!

CHAPTER 6

Now is the time

Why people want brands to *come from somewhere*

Many companies have understood for many years how much value can be added to their brands through leveraging their real or perceived country of origin: and in a time when the products in the shops could come from almost anywhere, their country of origin, their rootedness, becomes ever more important to the consumer.

The reason must surely be that people find it easier to like and trust *real* brands, not synthetic constructs without a history or a home.

Many companies which, a decade ago, were rushing to create 'global' brands, are starting to see that however attractive a global brand might appear to the corporation and its shareholders, it's not something which consumers always care for.

As part of the process which leads to the vague nirvana of globalness, lots of companies have attempted systematically to remove every clue about their country of origin from their products and services. British Airways' fateful decision in 1997 to graduate from mere national carrier to global travel brand, drop the explicit reference to its country of origin and the Union Flag, and carry images from many different nations on its tailplanes, was one of several instances of this type. But in their rush to appear global, BA overlooked the crucial point that a global brand isn't a brand which comes from nowhere: in many of the most successful cases, it is a brand which may be *sold* everywhere, but *comes* from somewhere quite definite. Coca-Cola, Pepsi, McDonald's, Nike, Levi's, Timberland and Marlboro, for example, are only global brands by grace of the fact that they are most decidedly from America.

British Airways would never have become the world's favourite airline if it hadn't been, first and foremost, *British* airways: the age-old popular perception of 'brand Britain' (methodical, punctual, predictable, efficient, traditional, heritage-obsessed, class-ridden, status-driven, ceremonious, perhaps a bit boring), makes Britain the ultimate, the supremely logical country of origin for any brand in the business of air travel, hospitality and tourism. It's easy to be wise after the event, but by cutting off its connection with its home-brand, British Airways simply pulled the plug on its principal brand equity.

In 2001 the airline's new chief executive, Rod Eddington, an Australian, ordered the Union Jacks to be painted back on the planes. It often takes the objective viewpoint of an outsider to understand the essence of a nation's image.

It's not so surprising if people want brands to come from somewhere. After all, the first time you meet someone, it's human nature to ask them where they're from: and as the likelihood of that person coming from the same place as you do becomes smaller with every year that passes, the question becomes increasingly relevant.

A country of origin is *hard equity*, which in many cases doesn't need to be built from scratch, because it already exists in the consumer's mind, and has a definite shape and form.

There's no doubt that consumers are increasingly asking brands where they come from, and the correct answer is *not* 'wherever you want.' Many companies might just find that while they're burbling on about 'planet earth' or 'around the world', the consumer has gone away in search of something with a little more integrity.

The decline of Brand America and the Top Ten

The problem for Britain, America and their wealthy colleagues is that coming from one of the Top Ten countries no longer carries quite the same cachet as it once did. America, in particular, is currently undergoing certain changes to the way it is perceived abroad which could signal a long-term decline in its brand equity.

The principal equity of brand America was always *freedom*, which is why it was so potent during the 1940s, 1950s and 1960s. For people emerging from the shadow of fascism, communism or simply a rather strait-laced bourgeois capitalism, the notion of a country where cowboys roamed free, went to bed when they wanted, drank coffee at all hours and never washed behind their ears, seemed like nirvana. America was a place where the kids, not the grown-ups, were in charge.

But freedom itself is a commodity with far less scarcity value today in the rest of the West – today, most Europeans know, have and are entirely familiar with personal liberty.

The absolutely compelling imagery of fashion brands from America is undoubtedly one of the most enduring stories of the success of Brand USA, and is intimately linked with the captivating notion of freedom: alongside Coke and Marlboro, iconic global lifestyle brands such as Levi's, Nike, Timberland, Lucky Strike, Pepsi, Wrangler and Lee are America's most accessible and most successful 'carry-out' – for nearly a century, these brands have been the wearable, affordable slice of American freedom which young consumers worldwide can take away from a Hollywood or Motown experience.

For decades, young consumers in Europe have been using such brands to claim their own patch of territory in the American Dream. Moreover, American products were, for a long time, simply better made, more attractive and more sensibly priced than European products. Small wonder that for many, many years, American brands have merely had to state their country of origin in order to become market leaders in Europe and worldwide.

But we may have already passed the peak of Brand America's international appeal. The relentless communication of American values and beliefs and lifestyle through the mass media has achieved the probably undesired but entirely predictable effect of making foreigners very familiar with them – many millions of people, after decades of intense bombardment by American culture through cinema, music, television and brands, are now (or believe themselves to be) experts on America.

And familiarity breeds contempt: America is no longer a mysterious, idealised, far-off, magical land: it's a place which many of us know (or think we know) almost as well as our own countries. Furthermore, people travel more than they used to because it's cheaper and they have more leisure time, and more people than ever before have *been there*: it's just as cheap and easy for the average European parent to take their children to Disney World in Orlando than to Euro Disney in Paris. Somehow, America just doesn't feel so far away any more.

With familiarity also comes discernment. Current views of America around the world present a more complex and more contradictory picture than at any time in the past; there is much that is positive, and much that is negative in current perceptions of Brand USA. Much of this ambiguity is the inevitable consequence of America's position as sole global superpower, and people's attitudes to absolute dominion are always mixed and uneasy.

With rare exceptions, simply stating its country of origin is no longer enough to build an American brand abroad. America is no longer a premium brand, and the world's love affair with America isn't exactly over, but it's a love that's no longer blind and unquestioning. There is clearly no single other country which offers anything like the overall breadth and power of Brand USA, or its reputation for quality and consistency across so many different product and service areas, but several other countries now compete quite effectively in specific contexts.

Of course, a decline in the equity of America's brand doesn't mean the end of the country or of its export business: but it does signal the end of the 'unfair advantage' which it once gave to American exporters. In the future, American brands will have to compete with other countries' brands on a more level playing-field, on their intrinsic merits rather than on the lazy shorthand that they simply come from the right place. Indeed, should Brand USA slip far enough in people's esteem, there is a chance that American brands will one day have to work *harder* than others in order to undo the negative associations which their country of origin contributes, or else, like brands from poor countries today, they will need to conceal or disguise their true provenance. I'm certain that in some fields – such as accountancy – 'Made in America' is already negative equity.

And it's not just America whose brand values are in decline. Although the rest of the world has heard far less about the other Top Ten country brands, there are signs that consumers outside Europe are tiring of some of those old clichés too. The image of France, for example, as the ultimate 'quality of life' brand has been substantially eroded by its loss of primacy in many product areas – the new world wines cancelling much of the magic and mystique of French wines, Italian and American fashion and perfume labels lessening France's stranglehold on the luxury goods market, and the growing taste for lighter and more exotic food means that Italian, Chinese, Mexican, Japanese, American and Indian cooking are all jostling for France's traditional position as the leading world cuisine. Germany's quality manufacturing image, Britain's heritage image, and Switzerland's precision and integrity image have all taken a battering in similar ways during the last decades.

And here lies the most exciting opportunity for brands from emerging markets. In purely branding terms, there are great gaps in the global palette of country-brands for countries which are 'about' qualities other than power, wealth and sophistication: perhaps creativity, philosophy, diversity, tolerance, trust, innocence, wisdom, challenge, risk, safety and who knows what else besides.

Western consumers and the search for exoticism

During the last decade, there has been a pronounced shift in Western tastes and fashions towards 'Asianisation' – a yearning for the values of older, wiser, more contemplative civilizations than our own.

Never before has there been such a vogue for the 'ethnic', the organic, the exotic. World music, ethnic art, global cinema and theatre, multicultural advertising, tribal fashion, fusion cuisine, Eurasian architecture, oriental design, Eastern religion, alternative medicine and the new world literature: the Western consumer is attracted as never before by the cultures and the products of distant lands.

You can see the trend in the food that people eat.

A 2001 report from market analysts Datamonitor, *Future Food Flavours*, finds that consumers are attracted as never before to exotic tastes. The variety of ethnic ready meals and cooking sauces is expanding at a rapid rate across Europe and the US; Cajun and fusion food are becoming more and more popular as consumers seek excitement for their taste buds and what the survey calls 'a real flavours explosion'.

The survey also notes that consumers are becoming more demanding and discerning about the real or perceived authenticity of the 'ethnic' food they buy, rather than products with a 'manufactured spin'. Even highly prepared food such as ready meals and cooking sauces need to emphasize their authenticity, and consumers appear not to be troubled at all by this apparent contradiction.

Much of the phenomenon is ascribed to ever greater numbers of people returning from ever more exotic holiday locations, expressing their desire to recreate the flavours they encounter abroad. Not only are increased proportions of the European and North American population travelling, but there has also been a striking diversification in the places they are visiting over the last decades. The Datamonitor report quotes the 1998 International Passenger Survey which shows that trips to Asia, North Africa, Latin America and the Caribbean by British visitors have grown at a compound annual rate of 100 per cent since 1990.

Not surprisingly, the travel statistics are mirrored in the products which can be found in supermarkets back home in Europe and North America, especially within the ready meals sector. Food from the Asia Pacific region, and Thai food in particular, is extremely popular, and this can be partly ascribed to the attraction of the region to young backpackers. Presumably some of this food is not just sold to the returning travellers who want to recreate their food experiences, but also to a proportion of would-be travellers who can indulge some of their curiosity about distant lands without actually having to find the time, money and courage to go there.

And you can see the trend in the music that people are listening to.

'When we started MTV Asia in 1992, only one Asian video had been made,' says MTV chairman and chief executive Thomas Freston. 'So we played that, and everything else was basically American. Today, we have MTV China, and 80 to 90 per cent of the videos we run there are made in China and sung in Chinese ... World music is still very small, but it's 20 times bigger than it was a couple of years ago: it hasn't reached mass market potential yet, but I regard that as an inevitability.'[51]

Gerald Seligman, head of Artist & Repertoire at EMI Records Europe in 2000, commented:

> Figures are hard to come by, though it is demonstrably true that those former repertoire powerhouses, the US and UK, now represent less of the overall worldwide music sales than they have in decades. Regional artists are selling more each year ... in the UK – and this is typical of Europe and North America in general – world music is the fastest-growing section of retail. Both HMV and Virgin Megastore report roughly 40% increases in sales year on year.

All this is good news for artists and record companies in emerging markets, just as the changes in food buying habits are good news for the food producers and exporters. But the broader implications are far more significant: what it implies is a major shift in taste.

It feels like a particularly good moment for the rightful owners of the truly exotic nation brands to leverage the power they hold over the imagination of the world's richest consumers. Now is the time for them to start making back some of the money which they have paid rich countries for their products over the past century, to begin to reverse the relentless flow of wealth from poor to rich, and to redress some of the imbalance between the lucky and the unlucky nations.

In my 'Eleven Levers for outsmarting the competition' in Chapter 4, I defined Lever No. 8 as 'Leveraging Social Change':

> The brands which achieve the greatest success are those which, by accident or design, find themselves in the path of major social change. ... Much of the art of brand strategy, therefore, is about the ability to put one's ear to the ground, like an Indian hunter, and hear when the bison are about to change direction and stampede in any particular direction.

I could extend the observations about changing consumer tastes beyond food and music to cover almost any area of any Northern marketplace at this moment, but it is hardly necessary: the indications are clear.

The restless bison are pawing the ground, and are already beginning to move.

A taste for ethics

Running parallel to the desire for more 'exotic' ideas and products is a rapidly growing consciousness among consumers in the North that, in a globalized world, the act of purchase is not private and isolated, but connected through a long and complex chain to many people, many countries, and many consequences.

This reassurance that the consequences of purchase are benign and transparent is an extra 'brand ingredient' which is rapidly becoming a focus of consumer demand in many countries. The phenomenon will continue to be helped by the anti-corporate movement and the growing trend for consumers to evaluate brands and the producers of brands according to their corporate citizenship credentials; and the exposure of dishonest practice among major corporations is part of this too. A US survey in August 2002 found that 68 per cent of people were less likely to trust everyday brands as a result of the unscrupulous actions of Enron and WorldCom;[52] it is an absolute certainty that these people are now more than usually sensitive to messages from companies which look and feel as different as possible from the classic US-owned multi-national.

The fact that the disgraced corporations are, so far, all American, also contributes to the erosion of brand America in other parts of the world – if it is America's economic might and commercial primacy which lies at the heart of the rest of the world's unease about the country, then any suggestion that this primacy has been dishonestly achieved is bound to cause huge disaffection.

This set of circumstances represents an urgent opportunity for our emerging-market brands to take a great leap forward.

After all, what better ethical purchase could one wish for than a product which is born ethical – one that is entirely conceived, manufactured and shipped directly by a locally-owned company in a developing market? The attraction of such a simple and transparent chain of consequences is the knowledge that such products create a *direct line of income* from consumer to producer – one that is far more direct than aid via taxes or charities. By buying a branded product from an emerging market, the consumer in a developed country directly funds the growth of the company from his or her wallet.

Naturally, there is a heavy burden on the manufacturer to prove that money spent on the product will be used wisely and well, to benefit the wider community as well as just the owner of the factory: but this may well form part of the brand's 'story' and help to build its special magic.

The fate of companies and their products used to hinge on the old model of product supremacy: with its consequent demands for ever greater manufacturing volume and quality, this model favoured the first world, and built the first world. But the new model includes a bigger and bigger element of emotional or brand supremacy: this model favours the second and third worlds. The developing world is where the great brands will come from – the great storehouse of emotional, cultural, intellectual and spiritual brand qualities.

My first 'Lever for Outsmarting the Competition' talked about the importance of changing the context in which brands compete with each other, and effectively 'moving the battleground' to one which suits the challenger to market leadership better than its suits the incumbent. Emerging brands from developing markets have a unique potential to make the Northern-owned superbrands look very grubby indeed, and their protestations of moral and ethical purity very suspect. And this can – and should – be done without it being necessary to make ethics a primary component of their brand values. Of course, under scrutiny or when requested, the brands must have spotless credentials and their owners and funding governments likewise. But social responsibility should be their context and natural domain, rather than their message.

Ethical qualifications, like trendiness in youth brands, is something which feels like a lie the moment you say it. You have to *prove* it rather than talk about it, and let people make their own conclusions.

Until quite recently, most 'ethical' purchases available to consumers were based on a single, simple philanthropic principle: the brand stood for a guarantee that farmers and manufacturers had been paid a stable, somewhat inflated market rate for their products. This basic FairTrade-type model, laudable though it is in so many respects, has one problem, in that the chief brand equity on which it's based is sympathy. If it works, it works because it plays on the guilt or anger or sense of charity of the consumer, and makes a spectacle out of the weakness of the producers, and the unfair way in which they are treated. This aspect is written right into the DNA of the concept – it's called *fair*, as opposed to *unfair*, trade.

This is bound to be pretty effective with a minority of highly motivated consumers, but it's basically an act of politics rather than marketing. No problem there, you might say, but in marketing terms it is a dead-end strategy: all the model does is shift the dependence of certain producers away from 'cynical' buyers to 'ethical' buyers, but doesn't provide the producer with a robust, protected, long-term benefit.

In other words, it's not truly sustainable: in fact, it may damage the brand in the long run, because it's so unlikely that consumers would ever be prepared to reframe a brand in their own minds from one which they feel they *ought* to buy to one which they actually *want* to buy.

The producers of the commodities being sold, moreover, aren't building up any brand equity of their own – they are simply preferred suppliers to a first-world brand-owner. In this sense, the model isn't radical at all, just a well-intentioned variant of the traditional supplier/brand-owner relationship.

In the end, if a company is looking for long-term loyalty from its consumers, the ability to preserve a substantial profit margin and rapid acceptance of new products on the marketplace, this has to be driven by something more self-interested than their moral principles. Whether we like it or not, the most predictable, most durable, most reliable and most consistent human motive on which to base a business is 'what's in it for *me?*' People will only reliably buy products from a company – and continue to buy that company's products – if they *want* them.

There is a wise saying in Italian which translates as 'he who makes himself a sheep will get eaten by the wolf' – in other words, it is human nature to strike at the weak. Many consumers, in many situations, seem to prefer brands they can look up to rather than look down on: they want to feel that the brand has qualities they can aspire to.

For all these reasons, the fair-trade brands are becoming visibly more 'commercial' and concentrating far more on product quality than before. The products sold in the UK by **Café Direct**, one of the pioneers of the field, are now in terms of packaging design, positioning, marketing and price, almost indistinguishable from their non-ethical peers. They now even market a highly successful freeze-dried instant coffee, a sophisticated product targeted at younger upmarket consumers which is worlds away from the basic, rather pious ethical offerings of the early 1990s. The ethical story functions as a key support to the other brand equities – quality and price – rather than being the primary equity itself, and if a brand wants to acquire mass-market volume, that's what it has to do.

The simple fact is that most people spend their hard-earned money rather sporadically on charitable causes: but *everybody* spends money on themselves day in, day out.

The Shared Equity Model

A different approach to the problem is the Shared Equity Model, a concept devised by Paul Weatherly. The idea is that coffee and other commodity farmers and producers, either individually or through group enterprises, own a share of equity in the brands that market their commodities.

Both Shared Equity and Fair Trade try to improve the lot of poor farmers by modifying the traditional model of trade in commodities. But the two approaches differ both in their view of the causes of poverty and in their proposed solutions; they also differ in their approach to marketing.

Fair Trade considers low commodity prices to be the cause of third world poverty and pays poor farmers a minimum price for the *products of their labour*. In effect, Fair Trade asks marketing companies (and consumers) to pay a voluntary, 'conscience' tax to producers as a subsidy; and, very laudably, it makes do with smaller profits than traditional coffee marketers in order to protect the margins of its producers. Weatherly argues that this approach is inherently contrary to the principles of the free market because it attempts to insulate small farmers from the market forces which cause low and unstable commodity prices.

It's no accident that the non-profit, non-governmental organizations which advocate Fair Trade – such as Oxfam, which owns a quarter of Café Direct – are almost all philosophically opposed to globalization and free trade.

Coffee is a good example of how Shared Equity can operate. The model doesn't require marketers, such as coffee roasters, to raise their input cost in order to pay producers a minimum wage. On the contrary, it encourages them to take profit-maximizing decisions by offering them the incentive of growth in overall sales. Having equity that is valued in developed world capital markets gives farmers more options than getting a higher price for a commodity does: for example, they can use their shares as collateral for a loan to invest in education or other ways to earn income. According to de Soto's argument (which I mentioned in Chapter 2), what the poor lack is negotiable proxies for capital: a stake in the brand under which their products are marketed provides them with just this.

Coffee is just one example of an industry where many small farmers actually need to stop production because they are not competitive. By contrast, Fair Trade's subsidy keeps small farmers from even recognizing that they should be thinking about escape routes from the trap of the commodity market.

The Wild Coffee Project

The Wild Coffee Project is Weatherly's first working example of the Shared Equity Model.[53] It's a business which is intended to create a mutually beneficial relationship between the Kibale National Park in Uganda – a fragile ecosystem with endangered forest elephants, 11 species of primates, and numerous species of birds, butterflies and plants – and the communities surrounding the park.

The project aims to market a brand of coffee in the United States and elsewhere as a way of earning income for the park and communities, and to fund community development and conservation programs in and around the park.

But Kibale National Park is a protected area of natural, native vegetation, not a coffee-producing zone of farms. The point about the Wild Coffee Project is not primarily to sell wild coffee, but to manage the natural ecosystem by encouraging the harvesting of wild coffee only within scientifically derived controls and limits, and to *save* wild coffee through a cause-related brand.

This approach does not, of course, spell volume production, and direct sales of wild coffee could never generate enough income to fulfil the project's objectives. At a Fair Trade price, the total wild coffee harvest in 2001 would have yielded less than $1 500. This isn't enough money to run the harvest programme: it wouldn't even pay for the wild coffee certification process, and it's certainly not enough to give the thousands of people in Kibale a better standard of living. To generate $1 million in income – enough to save the park and bring meaningful change in the state of development of local communities – would mean selling Wild Coffee for around a thousand dollars per pound, a price which, of course, nobody in their right mind would pay.

Instead, the idea is to make Wild Coffee into a sought-after ingredient brand, which, blended with other coffees, markets a commercially viable quantity of the brand at a reasonable price. The consumer benefit isn't taste, or even quality – in such small proportions, it isn't going to make much difference to the product – but it does have a big effect on the 'consumer experience'. This is coffee without the bitter aftertaste.

What the Kibale project and Café Direct's latest products both suggest is that the brand equities of 'ethical' and 'premium' will not be incompatible for very much longer. This is a hopeful development for some producers in the third world, who, with the right kind of marketing help, may find that they don't have to depend on the consumer's charity in order to charge a higher price for their produce.

Tiny projects like Kibale, and even larger-scale operations like Café Direct, are not on their own going to make a difference to the vast majority of subsistence producers in the third world: a few enterprising farmers who are lucky enough to attract the attention and support of enlightened and marketing-savvy development thinkers may eventually find their way out of the poverty trap, but in the general scheme of things the effect is vanishingly small. And it couldn't be otherwise: the marketplaces of the first world have, ultimately, a limited capacity for premium brands.

This is absolutely not a reason for people to stop proposing and building such schemes, of course – as I have said before, the ocean is made of drops, and the history of major social change has often been the history of lots of people doing lots of small things. The combination of big vision and untiring, tiny actions, as evidenced by the best development projects, deserves unstinting praise. But the *example* which such schemes afford, if well publicized, is almost more valuable than the individual schemes themselves: it inspires others and plays a part in tipping the balance from a basically selfish moral climate in business to a basically kind one.

What's more, niche branding exercises like Wild Coffee and some of the brands I described in Chapter 3 may prove to be the tip of a larger iceberg. These are businesses based on a handful of variants on the general theme of premium international export brands from poorer countries, but there is undoubtedly a much wider range of global market 'plays' which such producers could make: different business models, different distribution approaches, different market strategies, different relationships with Northern companies, and so on. With enough business models, there is little danger that rich-country markets could become saturated with emerging-market brands.

However, for major change to occur, big things have to happen too, or the ocean will simply take too long to fill. Business as a whole – not merely the companies which have some ethical purpose in their makeup, but all businesses – easily possess the bulk and power to alter the values of entire populations. If the brand values of a mere hundred companies are worth more money than 40 per cent of what the world's population earns in a year, and if one brand can turn entire continents on to new behaviours, like keeping fit or drinking more milk or wearing seat-belts, then it is clear that these corporations could create substantial changes in the distribution of global wealth with relative ease.

If the business model of a Café Direct or a Wild Coffee Project – or even a diluted form of it – were to become the standard for corporations like Pepsi or Nestlé or Wal-Mart, real global change would happen quite quickly.

I said before that consumers can only be relied upon to behave in a consistently ethical way if there is an element of simple self-interest combined with appeals to their principles, and the same is even more true of corporations. The publicly-owned ones in particular are self-interested by statute and by design, so it is likely to require somewhat more than a conscientious CEO to cause them to change their behaviours or – most effective of all, and correspondingly least likely to occur – make do with smaller profits.

Consumers are the only higher authority which big corporations recognize, so if consumers began to demand that all their products were ethically produced and sold by responsible companies, this would be sufficient to create change. To a degree, this is already happening, because it is now firmly part of the 'spirit of the age' that a benign and caring brand image is considered to be a basic requirement for all companies. The fact that many companies are visibly competing against each other to be recognized as more benign and more caring is a good sign that this is occurring.

However, it's still not pure self-interest either on the part of the consumers creating the demand, or the corporations responding to it. It might just be a passing fad, a reaction to the rather cynical and mercenary spirit of the 1980s (although I rather doubt it). More likely, it might reach a peak and then fall into decline as it is taken for granted and as consumers lose interest in the freshness of the debate. A newer, younger, angrier generation of consumers will inevitably come along, react against the caring attitude of their parents and seek out values and behaviours as opposite from them as they can find.

A reason to hope for a more robust change in behaviour is that there happens to be a strong argument of self-interest here too: many big companies, as a result of their size and their growth imperative, are simply running out of consumers. Second and third-world development is essential if these companies are to continue to grow, and their interest is not too hard to reconcile with a recognizably moral one: they need consumers who are wealthy enough to buy their products, have enough free time to enjoy them, are educated enough to consume advertising messages and evaluate products and brands, and live in countries where there is the liberty to make money and spend it.

A good example of how corporate self-interest can be wholly reconciled with ethical purpose – and not merely disguised as it – comes from Hewlett-Packard. HP's e-inclusion programme, which is working with other companies, governments and NGO's to improve access to clean water, food, health, education and reliable political and economic infrastructure in poor and developing markets, is acknowledged inside the corporation to be less a social initiative than a simple response to the company's long term business self-interest.

As Joe Podolsky, a marketing manager at HP says, technology companies like HP have a limited marketplace for their products: like most of their competitors, HP can only sell to about 2 billion of the world's population of 6 billion, and these are concentrated mostly in Western Europe, North America, and the eastern coasts of Asia. If HP and other producers of more expensive or sophisticated products and services are to continue to grow in the next decades, they simply have to find ways of creating consumers, business partners, and employees among those currently unserved 4 billion.

So providing food, water, health, education and democracy (or something like it) to the 4 billion may look like social initiative, but it really comes from a deep understanding of future markets and resources. And as Joe Podolsky freely admits, for a publicly owned business, that's a much more reliable motive than altruism. The language which HP itself uses publicly to describe the e-inclusion programmes is also refreshingly free of ethical cant. On its website, the company lists the four main reasons why it is undertaking the programme as follows:

1. to establish HP as a leader in an exciting new technology growth area that also demonstrates our character and commitment to social contribution;
2. to create significant revenue and profit growth over time through the creation of new markets, products and services;
3. to provide a showcase to the world of our capabilities in terms of devices, infrastructure and services;
4. to enhance current HP business opportunities in emerging markets.[54]

As more and more corporations make more and more urgent appeals to consumers to consider them ethical and transparent, there is a real chance that such arguments will begin to replace the kind we are currently seeing. Most big companies would like us to believe that they are kind and caring because that's just the way they are, and as long as it's only a small minority of companies talking in this way, it's possible that some consumers will believe them. But pretty soon, people will be looking for more convincing arguments, and although it's less gracious and less appealing for a company to state that its responsible behaviour is pure self-interest, it is ultimately far more believable – and it has the enormous advantage of being a message which can be communicated without modification or concealment or fear of overspill to consumers and shareholders alike.

But these arguments and everything which I've described in this book so far have one thing in common: the consequence of all of them is a great and growing volume of international trade, and the shipment of ever more goods over ever greater distances.

It's essential to pause for a moment and consider whether this is actually a desirable outcome. As Helena Norberg-Hodge says:[55]

> The most urgent issue today, however, isn't whether people have oranges in cold climates but whether their wheat, eggs or milk should travel thousands of miles when they could be produced within a fifty-mile radius. In Mongolia, a country that has survived on local milk products for thousands of years and that today has twenty-five million milk-producing animals, one finds mainly German butter in the shops. In Kenya, butter from Holland is half the price of local butter; in England, butter from New Zealand costs far less than the local product; and in Spain, dairy products are mainly Danish. In this absurd situation, individuals are becoming dependent for their everyday needs on products that have been transported thousands of miles, often unnecessarily. The goal of localization would not be to eliminate all trade but to reduce unnecessary transport while encouraging changes that would strengthen and diversify economies at both the community and national levels.

A speech given in January 2002 in London by the Indian activist and academic, Vandana Shiva,[56] ended with 'a global demand that imports be controlled by governments and that exports should only consist of genuine surplus leftovers after food security needs have been met at all levels by domestic production. "Let the world food trade deal in the leftovers!" '

The 'localist' point of view is an attractive and comforting one at first glance – the notion that countries can fare better if they are allowed to be self-sufficient – and it is all too easy to produce examples of international trade which appear farcical, outrageous, even obscene. But in reality, this is classic Luddism – the predictable reaction against any development which offends the logic of previous generations. I'm quite certain that when produce was first shipped fifty miles by train from one city to another, shrill voices were raised, claiming that such extravagance was entirely unnecessary, against nature, and asking for trouble. Yes, on the face of it, it does seem absurd that food which comes from far away is cheaper than stuff produced locally, but if you *do* have a global world, then shipping products around the global neighbourhood is normal and to be expected. It's part of the consequence of consumers and markets constantly searching for the best combination of value and quality.

It's also one of the consequences of the death of distance. A generation ago, it would have been considered absurd to travel from London to New York for an hour's meeting and come home the same day, but because technology makes it possible, situations soon emerge which make it necessary, and thus it happens. That's the way of the world and the nature of progress. If massive, complex and occasionally eccentric movement of goods is what is required in order to create and preserve a *fair* worldwide balance of wealth, then so be it. Of course, if starving people are exporting produce instead of eating it, that needs to be addressed. But very often, people who object to trade are doing so simply on the grounds that they can't see the sense of it.

If a rather odd distribution of certain products were the only cost of increased global trade, we wouldn't have such a serious problem.

But we do have a serious problem. Increased trade, and the economic development which accompanies it, could easily destroy the planet.

The riddle of sustainability

A decade ago, around 1 700 of the world's leading scientists, including most of the Nobel prize-winning scientists, issued the following warning to humanity:

> Human beings and the natural world are on a collision course ... No more than one or a few decades remain before the chance to avert the threats we now confront will be lost and the prospects for humanity immeasurably diminished.[57]

The first of those decades has already passed since the extraordinary pronouncement was made, and humanity continues on its usual course, with the good work being done in the cause of sustainability comfortably outweighed by continuing and worsening pollution elsewhere.

So the question which arises at the end of *Brand New Justice* isn't really how or whether the emerging world can catch up with the first, using the same tools as the first, but the realization that the poor and developing countries must surpass the industrialized countries by finding routes to growth which not only pollute substantially less (and create sustainable ways of enjoying their new prosperity), but also, in the process, help to repair some of the damage that the North has done during its own long phase of growth.

Obviously, it is partly the responsibility of the developed nations to develop and transfer the technology which will enable this miracle to happen, but one has to consider carefully what the poor actually *want* and are prepared to take from the rich. Bunker Roy, the director of India's Barefoot College, made the point at the 2002 Summit of the World Technology Network at the United Nations,[58] that smart European or American graduates suddenly appearing in villages in the third world, armed with inappropriate advice, boundless enthusiasm and very limited relevant experience, can often be worse than unhelpful: Roy stresses the value of South-to-South collaboration, which, he says, is likely to be more immediately applicable, more relevant, and more sensitive.

And the question remains of the *willingness* of the recipients of this technology and advice, no matter where it comes from: what will ensure that countries desperate for rapid growth don't simply reach for the quickest, cheapest and least environmentally-friendly routes to prosperity they can find?

It certainly sounds like the worst kind of hypocrisy when the developed nations, comfortably enjoying the prosperity which is the direct result of centuries of thoughtless waste and profligacy with our natural resources, insist that poor countries behave better than they did. And it would be entirely consistent with human nature if the developing countries simply ignored the request.

One human factor which might prove useful is the opportunity which this situation affords to companies and governments in the 'new world' to show their moral and ethical superiority in being newer, cleaner, more modern and more responsible than the dirty old 20th-century capitalist and industrialist economies. The rise of the South might just be very different from the rise of the North – more prudent, more wise, a growth which occurs in harmony with the natural world rather than wielded savagely against it.

And in the developed world, what will ensure that consumers change the demands they make on industry to keep on supplying products and services which are so dangerous to the environment?

It would indeed be a massive shift if the West learned how to make do with less. After decades of encouragement and training by corporations, by the media, by the whole moral current of the age, to want more, bigger, better, faster, sooner and cheaper, is it likely that we could learn to aspire to products which offer slightly *less* than we are used to? Or even not *too* much more? Cars which aren't quite so fast, products which aren't quite so shiny, food which isn't quite so cheap and perfect, buildings which aren't quite so cold in warm weather? It seems like absolute cultural anathema.

Some have such unerring faith in the ingenuity of scientists that they believe technology can continue, more or less forever, to absorb the burden of lower emissions, greener materials, sustainable production, reduced waste and environmentally-friendly practice, while still maintaining regular improvements in the power, sophistication, attractiveness and desirability of their products. And perhaps they're right: generally, the profit imperative has always provided companies and inventors with the necessary motivation to perform such miracles.

But by the same token, the greener products won't be developed unless consumers demand them, and this is where the real sea-change needs to occur. The biggest task facing mass communications at this point in history is the need to fully establish in the minds of all consumers the desirability of sustainable consumption and sustainable behaviour: to make what is *sensible* as attractive as what is *desirable*, and to make this effect permanent.

There are many who claim that advertising and marketing are unequal to such a task: the official line of the advertising industry is that advertising is sometimes very good at reflecting existing beliefs and values but is quite unable to alter them. In a recent publication commissioned by the United Nations Environmental Program,[59] the World Federation of Advertisers makes its case for what it believes it can offer the cause of sustainability. The voluminous report is a funny mixture of an evidently sincere desire to help, and constant disclaimers about the extremely limited power of advertising to achieve anything of value to society. It opens on a very positive note, stating that 'advertising contributes to all three pillars of sustainable development: economic development, environmental protection and social responsibility' but ends with the all-too-familiar protestations of the marketing industry when under attack: 'There seems to us to be little prospect of altering lifestyles to suit the needs of sustainability through advertising. This must start in schools and be reflected in the values of society as a whole. At best advertising can only support and encourage values which are inherent in society'.

The point about sustainability starting in schools is well made, but the rest is too modest by far. The techniques of creative mass advocacy, as practised by the most successful brands, have a power to influence the behaviour of huge numbers of people in a way which is unequalled by almost any other force on the planet. Certainly, it's not what advertising usually does, because in the typical business model, advertising is used in a strictly limited way to promote the interests of a paying client. But the tools and techniques of persuasion which advertising uses to promote brands have a power which is limited only by the brief it's given. Yes, it's true that advertising can't make people buy something which they don't want; but if it's possible to prove that it's worth having, advertising can make them want it.

In any case, even if it were true that all advertising ever does is reflect existing or nascent trends in society, then sustainability is certainly a brief which it can answer, because the trend is so clearly apparent. A quick glance at the rapid adoption of CSR principles by most of the ad agencies' own clients, at the growth in ethical purchasing by the consumers which ad agencies study so closely, or simply at the increasing amounts of media time given over to sustainability issues (in between the spots which the agencies are buying for their clients), should be sufficient to make it abundantly clear that this particular nascent trend is considerably overdue. The advertising industry should get reflecting, and get on with it quick.

The sustainability brief is undoubtedly a rather bigger one than ad agencies are usually given by their clients. In point of fact, it's as big as religion, and there are plenty of links and parallels between the two.

It's the human condition to crave submission to higher authorities, and yet to do away with them as soon as we have them – one after another, this is what we in the North have done with our gods, politicians, monarchies and aristocracies; it's what each succeeding generation does with its parents and teachers. We constantly fall into the error of thinking that we are clever and powerful enough to stand on our own, but as soon as we have thrown down the temple and seen the empty vault of heaven above our heads, we go mad with terror.

In many ways, the cause of sustainability plays a similar role to a god in the human value-system. The need to save the planet is a new, higher, more urgent truth than the codes of moral and ethical behaviour and social contracts which were our guides in a world which still seemed to have a long future ahead of it. Sustainability presents a new and absolute set of 'commandments' to replace the religions we have destroyed and neglected, and to overlay with a new emphasis on the religions which still flourish.

But, appropriately for a scientific age, this religion is an empirical rather than a spiritual one, mapped out by science and based on experiment and observation. Just like religion, though, it provides a few, simple, enormous, existential and unavoidable truths about our salvation, which we can neither doubt, ignore, question nor escape. These basic commandments feed down into and nourish, justify and sustain the more complex social contracts and moral frameworks which lie beneath them and direct our everyday actions: and should these be called into question, the basic commandments are the ultimate moral backstop which confirms the general thrust of the system and keeps it on track should people become lost in a maze of detailed enquiry.

The most successful religions have been brilliantly effective and creative campaigns of mass communications: just like marketing campaigns, the great religions have taken complex issues and made them compelling, memorable and relevant to large numbers of uneducated people, using the power of language, striking visual imagery and potent symbolism. They have used 'soft power' to implant the necessary behaviours into society, and have fully understood that major changes in behaviour will only take place if they can be made aspirational; but a little hard power (by occasionally reminding people of the terrifying consequences of not complying) has almost always been a useful adjunct.

The sustainability campaign has, so far, made the usual mistake of all emergent movements, in allowing its righteous indignation to lead it to stress the hellfire and damnation too much, and the routes to salvation and causes for hope too little. There is nothing particularly new about the human instinct to wander away from preachers who do nothing but criticize and terrify their congregations, and the tendency to simply give up if things seem too bleak. People need a measure of hope on which to build their actions, and no matter how urgent the task, they need to be wheedled, charmed and cajoled into compliance.

I would suggest that the best way to effect a planetary conversion to sustainability would be by following the best religious models: nothing less would achieve the desired effect. This can't really be done without marketing, even if marketing is not what one chooses to call it: nonetheless, within the media disciplines there are sufficiently powerful tools to create the necessary groundswell and 'value shift' across many cultures, age-groups and levels of wealth.

Harnessing the huge bulk and influence of the world's corporations to this end is necessary and quite possibly sufficient to achieve the moral and philosophical sea-change which will redirect a meaningful proportion of humanity's energies towards the most pressing tasks which now face us. Of this I am certain.

The new question which the world needs to be taught to ask itself is, like all profound truths, apparently rather simple. I have never heard it more succinctly expressed than by John Perry Barlow, a retired Wyoming cattle-rancher and sometime lyricist of the Grateful Dead, at the 2002 Summit of the World Technology Network:

Consider what it means to be a good ancestor.

Tourism and sustainability – another challenge

The tourist industry is central to the debate about nation-brands and sustainable development.

I mentioned that tourism is often the primary stakeholder in promoting the national brand, and that the two are sometimes confused. This is because tourist promotion is usually the only way in which countries ever consciously engage in marketing themselves to the outside world: it is just about the only area of activity where, traditionally, a government minister and a director of marketing will actually work side by side, and it's often one of the few areas where the division between public sector and private enterprise is unclear.

What I have mainly described in this book are ways of taking emerging-market products to rich consumers. Tourism represents, among other things, a way to bring the rich consumers to the emerging-market products. The reality is that you need to do both, and they need to work together.

But both have to be done in a sustainable and responsible way. Tourism is the world's biggest industry, and has a unique potential to create wholesale and irreversible ecological damage to the planet. The need to manage and grow the industry in a sustainable way is overwhelmingly urgent. It's not difficult to find hair-raising examples of the direct ecological impact of tourism, and two are probably sufficient to make the point: the first is the fact that an average golf course in a tropical country needs 1 500 kg of chemical fertilizers, pesticides and herbicides per year and uses as much water as 60 000 rural villagers.[60] The second is the study which found that a single cruise ship anchor dropped in a coral reef for one day resulted in an area about half the size of a football field completely destroyed, and half as much again that died later as a result of being covered by rubble. It is estimated that the coral would take fifty years to recover from the incident.[61]

Part of the problem is that there are, as yet, few universally-acknowledged and dependable sets of standards to guide resorts, developers and consumers: and there is still far too much 'green-style' tourism on the market, just as there are far too many 'organic-style,' 'eco-style' and 'ethical-style' products. A good deal of what is billed as 'eco-tourism' is the exact opposite of sustainable tourism: by taking large numbers of visitors into environmentally sensitive areas, it speeds their destruction.

If properly managed, however, tourism can be a highly effective way of persuading large numbers of people to change their priorities and consumption habits. To quote the UN Ecological Program, 'Tourism has the potential to increase public appreciation of the environment and to spread awareness of environmental problems when it brings people into closer contact with nature and the environment. This confrontation may heighten awareness of the value of nature and lead to environmentally conscious behavior and activities to preserve the environment.' In other words, it's far easier to persuade people of the importance of 'green' behaviour by showing them the endangered places than simply talking about it.

The enormous size of the tourism industry makes it a valuable ally in the cause of widespread behaviour change: the quantity of purchasing and transport and energy consumption which it generates (which is especially noticeable when it's in remoter or poorer areas because of the way these processes tend to dwarf the scale of indigenous industry), tourism has the power to make major changes and provide powerful examples to other industries as well as other consumers. Purchasers in tourism businesses can lead by example too: by refusing to deal with suppliers who don't conform to ecological standards and so on.

Tourism can create low-impact development, if imaginatively planned. UNEP gives the example of the Eco-escuela de Español, a Spanish language school created in 1996 as part of a Conservation International project in the village of San Andres in Guatemala. The school offers individual language courses, home stay opportunities and community-led eco-tours to around 1 800 mainly American and European tourists each year: it is owned and staffed by the villagers, and has helped to wean many of them off their previous pursuits – illegal timber extraction, hunting and slash-and-burn agriculture.

Travel broadens the mind and makes people more aware of the inter-connectedness of things – of the direct and indirect consequences of their consumption habits – and can make people more sensitive about their own environment back home. People can learn good habits from the tourism industry: even the now universal practice of hotels requesting guests not to put out all their towels for washing every day has made many people think a little harder about the impact of their everyday behaviour, as well as saving a great many hotels a great deal of money.

Once again, it is clear that threats are usually also opportunities, and that enormous bulk can be useful if its direction can be turned, the world's biggest industry can be the planet's biggest helper, or its worst enemy.

All industries need to search for these axes, the points of equilibrium where their power to harm can be converted into a power to do good. Without the power and influence of big business, there is little chance that anything will change except for the worse.

Some concluding thoughts

One of the things which this book has turned out to be is a defence of marketing. I hope I have shown that marketing is not the convenient scapegoat for the evils of consumerism or global capitalism which many would have it: the truth, as always, is more complex and contradictory than this.

I hope I have also shown that marketing is not about adding worthless gloss to worthless products, or persuading dumb consumers to waste money on rubbish they neither need nor want, nor is it a charlatan's trick for overcharging people for ordinary products. It is a way of squeezing more value out of a marketplace; a way of stimulating trade and commerce; and, in the right hands, an immensely powerful instrument for widespread social and cultural change.

It is in any case the unavoidable and necessary product of a free market economy: if nobody did marketing at all, we could perhaps do without it (although consumers would probably invent it sooner or later anyway). But since *some* people use it, it's the ones that don't who are simply at a disadvantage, and it is this disadvantage which I believe needs correcting.

Like many of us, my personal feeling is that the degree to which shopping values have become the dominant force in Western society is worrying: the atmosphere of commercialism and materialism is rapidly becoming stifling, and the principle which, in a very different but not very distant age, was simply known as greed, is now pre-eminent to a degree which simply doesn't seem healthy. Various writers have been unable to resist the pun that we are 'dying of consumption'. According to the Center for a New American Dream, a group which aims to promote sustainable behaviour, 'the traditional American Dream once focused on greater security, opportunity and happiness. Increasingly, that dream has been supplanted by an extraordinary emphasis on acquisition.'[62]

For 'American', one can easily substitute the name of any developed country without diminishing the truth of the observation. In such an environment, it is difficult for the more worthwhile products of the human spirit – that which is closest to the divine in each of us – such as culture, to survive untainted. Despite some of the ways in which I have tried to show how they can collaborate, culture and commerce don't sit happily together, and it sometimes looks as if the latter is literally killing off the former.

Commerce has its great strengths and its important uses – not least, it has been and continues to be the best route out of poverty for hundreds of millions of people – but culture is humanity's best defence against many other evils, including tyranny and war. By reminding us that we aspire to greater things than the satisfaction of our appetites, culture gives us the dignity and self-respect to improve as a species.

One could debate forever about whether marketing has knowingly contributed to the unequal distribution of global wealth, the rise of unsustainable and ecologically damaging manufacturing and consuming patterns, and the murder of culture. But let us be fair, and assume that marketing has been an accessory to the crime, and acted out of ignorance rather than wickedness. Now it must do its community service.

For this reason, I have no hesitation in proposing the principles of *Brand New Justice* as a piece of *realpolitik*. In an earlier chapter, I used the metaphor of martial arts to illustrate the wisdom of exploiting a heavy opponent's bulk and momentum to further one's own aims, and this vast juggernaut of greed and expenditure is a powerful beast: it simply doesn't make sense to contemplate ways of ending it or changing it.

Whether we personally like it or not, the dominant system is this potent form of materialistic capitalism which we in the West have created – it plays, undoubtedly, to powerful desires in all of us – and it is highly unlikely to change, go out of fashion, or stop growing in the near future. What does make sense is thinking about smart and subtle ways to work within the machine, and try to tip that vast bulk in a more fruitful direction. This is the natural environment for marketing, and there are few disciplines which better understand how to perform such tasks.

By helping gifted entrepreneurs and ambitious companies in poorer countries to develop the confidence and expertise to create and sell branded products and services in the rich markets of the North, marketing can stimulate their economic growth and build their competitive advantage.

By providing the governments of those poorer countries with the techniques to build a positive and powerful nation-brand, marketing can help to distribute the benefits of globalization more fairly, and make a real difference to the cultural and economic prospects of more than half the world.

By contributing its skills and experience to wean rich consumers off the wasteful and selfish ways which it has promoted and glamorized in the past, marketing can help to ensure that the world our children live in is not only fairer, but habitable too.

Who could ask for a more exciting or worthwhile challenge?

References

1. Source: Universal McCann. Quoted in *Industry As a Partner for Sustainable Development: Advertising:* World Federation of Advertisers (WFA), European Association of Communications Agencies (EACA) United Nations Environment Programme (2002).
2. IMD/PIMS: *A Virtuous Cycle: Innovation, Consumer Value, and Communication*, Commissioned by AIM European Brands Association (2000).
3. Scottish Enterprise: *Company Interviews and Bureau of Economic Analysis*, ICF Kaiser, quoted in *Global Companies Enquiry* (1999).
4. Joseph Nye: *The Paradox of American Power*, Oxford University Press (2002).
5. Hernando de Soto: *The Mystery of Capital*, Black Swan (2001).
6. According to Interbrand's 2001 survey, 93 per cent of Xerox's market value is attributable to goodwill.
7. Armando Sapori: *Studi di Storia Economica Medievale*, Florence (1946).
8. Edwin S Hunt: *The Medieval Super-Companies: A Study of the Peruzzi Company of Florence*, Cambridge University Press (1994).
9. World Trade Organization Committee on Trade and Development: 'Participation of Developing Countries in World Trade: Recent Developments and Trade of the Least-developed Countries' (Feb. 2000).
10. Quoted by Ronald Dore in *Making Sense of Globalisation*, London School of Economics – Centre for Economic Performance Working Paper No. 1096 (2000).
11. Raymond Blair: *E-procurement Makes Immediate Business Sense* (July 2001).
12. Reported in *Express Computer*, India (January 2002).
13. Michael Schrage: *Wal-Mart Trumps Moore's Law*, Technology Review (March 2002).
14. I am indebted to Paul Weatherly for allowing me to reproduce many of his arguments in the following section. Weatherly's *Shared Equity Model*, which provides a radical new approach to improving the profitability of third-world enterprises, is described in more detail in Chapter 6.

15. Patrick Knight: *Roasting the Competition*, Coffee & Cocoa International (December 2001).
16. Ian Batey: *Asian Branding*, Pearson Asia (2002).
17. Although the brand names are owned by American companies (Tropicana and Minute Maid, the market leaders, are owned by Pepsico and Coca-Cola respectively), the sharing of revenues between the USA and Brazil, and other orange producing countries, is somewhat more complex. Four of the five largest processing companies in São Paulo now own processing plants in Florida (this is partly a way of getting around import tariffs, partly a way of responding to the growth in demand for 'not-from-concentrate' juice, and partly a way of staying close to the all-important American customer). One of these companies, Cutrale, bought Minute Maid's processing plants, so while Minute Maid is still the number 2 orange juice *marketer* in the US, Cutrale is its main product supplier. Citrosuco, another Brazilian processor, has factories in Florida which make juice for Tropicana, and also produces Tropicana's Pure Premium, the world's largest not-for-concentrate brand, for the Argentine market. It's interesting how despite this close relationship, Tropicana scrupulously avoid making *any* reference to the fact that some of their juice is produced from Brazilian oranges – even on their fact-packed website, www.tropicana.com, which is full of declarations of the company's commitment to equal opportunities employment and promotion of 'the utilization of eligible Minority and Women Business Enterprises (M/WBE) in all aspects of the company's business'.
18. David Christopher Aldwinckle: *New Zealand's Economic Reforms – Were They Worth It?* in Hokkaido Information University *Memoirs* (i–v) Vol. 7. No. 2, pp. 45–60 (March 1996).
19. Tina Rosenberg: *The Free-Trade Fix*, NYTimes.com (18 August, 2002).
20. Ronald Dore: *Making Sense of Globalisation*, London School of Economics – Centre for Economic Performance Working Paper No. 1096 (2000).
21. C. Sautter: *Le Prix de la Puissance*, Paris, Le Seuil, (1973), and *Les Dents du Géant*, Paris, Olivier Orban (1987).
22. Michael I. Niman: *Branding Cuba: La Vida Nike*, AlterNet (14 May, 2002).
23. Kent Wertime: *Building Brands and Believers: How to Connect with Consumers Using Archetypes*, John Wiley and Sons (2002)
24. Thomas Crampton: *Thai Brands Seek to Upgrade Image – From Sweatshops to High Fashion* International Herald Tribune (2 March, 2000)
25. Elizabeth Florent-Treacy, Pavel Pavlovsky, Manfred Kets de Vries and Raoul de Vitry d'Avaucourt: *Case Study: Roustam Tariko: Russian Entrepreneur*, INSEAD (2000).

26. I am indebted to Prof. Janez Damjan of the University of Ljubljana for providing me with this information about Laško Pivo.
27. *Rough ride: Old names Have Lost Their Puff:* The Economist (1 June 2002).
28. Fons Trompenaars and Charles Hampden-Turner: *21 Leaders for the 21st Century,* Capstone (2001).
29. Actually, although many exporters do follow this model, it's seldom quite so straightforward. For a fuller discussion of the cultural and linguistic difficulties involved in marketing a product abroad, see my book *Another One Bites the Grass – Making Sense of International Advertising,* John Wiley and Sons, New York (2000).
30. The economic development and international business literature is full of suggestions about what countries can do to improve their investment climates. See Reuber *et al., Private Foreign Investment;* Sanjaya Lall and Paul Streeten, *Foreign Investment, Transnationals, and Developing Countries* (Boulder, Colorado: Westview Press, 1977); and Richard D. Robinson, *Foreign Investment in the Third World: A Comparative Study of Selected Developing Country Investment Promotion Programs* (Washington DC: Chamber of Commerce of the United States, 1980).
31. The most compelling of these is *The Tipping Point* by Malcolm Gladwell (Abacus, 2002).
32. I am indebted to Joakim Jonason, the creator of the Diesel advertising campaigns, for this example.
33. The principle of *smart centralization* is described in detail in my book, *Another One Bites the Grass*: Making Sense of International Advertising, John Wiley and Sons, New York (2000).
34. *Rigged Rules and Double Standards: Trade, Globalisation, and the Fight Against Poverty,* Oxfam (2002).
35. Jagdish Bhagwati: *The Poor's Best Hope,* The Economist (22 June, 2002).
36. This fact was noted by Russel Griggs, Executive Director of Scotland the Brand.
37. For a more detailed analysis of Brand America, see Simon Anholt: Brand USA – The Mother of All Brands, Cyan Books, London (2004).
38. Padadopoulos and Heslop: *Country Equity and Country Branding: Problems and Prospects,* The Journal of Brand Management, Vol. 9, No. 4–5, Simon Anholt (Ed.) (April 2002).
39. For example, see Eugene Jaffé and Israel Nebenzahl: *National Image and Competitive Advantage,* Copenhagen Business School Press (2001).
40. Quoted by Mark Leonard *et al.* in: *Public Diplomacy,* Foreign Policy Centre (2002).
41. Chris Powell: *How Cool is Britannia Now?* Chapter in *Heritage and Identity – Shaping the Nations of the North,* Donhead (2002).

42. Leclerc, Schmitt, Dubé: *Foreign Branding and Its Effect on Product Perceptions and Attitudes*, Journal of Consumer Research, Vol. 31 (1994).

43. Al Ries and Laura Ries, *The 11 Immutable Laws of Internet Branding*, Harper Business (2001).

44. Simon Anholt: *Another One Bites the Grass: Making Sense of International Advertising*, John Wiley and Sons, New York (2000).

45. Lanksy, Doug, *Last Trout in Venice*, Travelers' Tales Inc (2001).

46. I am indebted to Donhead Publishing for allowing me to reproduce parts of the following sections from a chapter which I contributed to *Heritage and Identity – Shaping the Nations of the North*, Donhead (2002).

47. MacDonald Royal Commission (Royal Commission, 1985, 115). Quoted in Harry Hillman Chartrand, *The Arts: Consumption Skills in the Post-Modern Economy* (Cultural Economics – Compiler Press).

48. Paul Temporal: *Why Asian Countries need Branding* on www. asiainc.com (2001).

49. John Pantzalis and Carl A. Rodrigues *Country Names as Brands – Symbolic Meaning and Capital Flows*, Montclair State University (1999).

50. Lars Gellerstad: Letter to the Author, August 2002.

51. Quoted by Justin Davidson in *Long Island/Queens: Our Future* (1999).

52. The research was sponsored by Madison-based branding firm Lindsay, Stone and Briggs, and AcuPOLL Precision Research. Source: Marketing Magazine.

53. See http://www.wildcoffee.org

54. Source: http://www.hp.com/e-inclusion/en/vision/faq.html

55. Helena Norberg-Hodge in *The Case Against The Global Economy*, Sierra Club (1997).

56. Reported in *Resurgence*, Issue 210.

57. *World Scientists' Warning to Humanity* (18 November 1992). Source: Union of Concerned Scientists.

58. See http://www.wtn.net

59. *Industry as a Partner for Sustainable Development: Advertising:* World Federation of Advertisers (WFA), European Association of Communications Agencies (EACA) United Nations Environment Programme (2002).

60. Source: http://www.tourismconcern.org.uk

61. Peter Benchley and Judith Gradwohl: *Ocean Planet: Writings and Images of the Sea*, Harry N. Abrams Inc., New York (1995).

62. Source: http://www.newdream.org

Index